RESUMES
FOR
GOVERNMENT
CAREERS

Professional Resumes Series

RESUMES FOR GOVERNMENT CAREERS

The Editors of VGM Career Horizons

Printed on recyclable paper

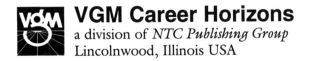

VGM Career Horizons
a division of *NTC Publishing Group*
Lincolnwood, Illinois USA

ACKNOWLEDGMENT

We would like to acknowledge the assistance of Mark Rowh in compiling and editing this book.

Library of Congress Cataloging-in-Publication Data

Resumes for government careers / the editors of VGM Career Horizons.
    p. cm.
    Includes bibliographical references.
    ISBN 0-8442-4158-x (paperback)
    1. Résumés (Employment)—United States. 2. Civil service Positions—
United States.   I. VGM Career Horizons (Firm)
JK716.R46 1996
808'.06665—dc20

96-3281
CIP

Published by VGM Career Horizons, a division of NTC Publishing Group
4255 West Touhy Avenue
Lincolnwood (Chicago), Illinois 60646-1975, U.S.A.
© 1996 by NTC Publishing Group. All rights reserved.
No part of this book may be reproduced, stored in a retrieval
system, or transmitted in any form or by any means,
electronic, mechanical, photocopying, recording or otherwise,
without the prior permission of NTC Publishing Group.
Manufactured in the United States of America.

6 7 8 9 0 VP 9 8 7 6 5 4 3 2 1

CONTENTS

Introduction   vii

Chapter One
The Elements of a Good Resume   1

Chapter Two
Writing Your Resume   15

Chapter Three
Assembly and Layout   19

Chapter Four
The Cover Letter   27

Chapter Five
Sample Resumes   31

Chapter Six
Sample Cover Letters   131

Introduction

Your resume is your first impression on a prospective employer. Though you may be articulate, intelligent, and charming in person, a poor resume may prevent you from ever having the opportunity to demonstrate your interpersonal skills, because a poor resume may prevent you from every being called for an interview. While few people have ever been hired solely on the basis of their resume, a well-written, well-organized resume can go a long way toward helping you land an interview. Your resume's main purpose is to get you that interview. The rest is up to you and the employer. If you both feel that you are right for the job and the job is right for you, chances are you will be hired.

A resume must catch the reader's attention yet still be easy to read and to the point. Resume styles have changed over the years. Today, brief and focused resumes are preferred. No longer do employers have the patience, or the time, to review several pages of solid type. A resume should be only one page long, if possible, and never more than two pages. Time is a precious commodity in today's business world and the resume that is concise and straightforward will usually be the one that gets noticed

Let's not make the mistake, though, of assuming that writing a brief resume means that you can take less care in preparing it. A successful resume takes time and thought, and if you are willing to make the effort, the rewards are well worth it. Think of your resume as a sales tool with the product being you. You want to sell yourself to a prospective employer. This book is designed to help you prepare a resume that will help you further your career—to land that next job, or first job, or to return to the work force after years of absence. So, read on. Make the effort and reap the rewards that a strong resume can being to your career. Let's get to it!

Chapter One

THE ELEMENTS OF A GOOD RESUME

A winning resume is made of the elements that employers are most interested in seeing when reviewing a job applicant. These basic elements are the essential ingredients of a successful resume and become the actual sections of your resume. The following is a list of elements that may be used in a resume. Some are essential; some are optional. We will be discussing these in this chapter in order to give you a better understanding of each element's role in the makeup of your resume:

1. Heading
2. Objective
3. Work Experience
4. Education
5. Honors
6. Activities
7. Certificates and Licenses
8. Professional Memberships
9. Special Skills
10. Personal Information
11. References

The first step in preparing your resume is to gather together information about yourself and your past accomplishments. Later you will refine this information, rewrite it in the most effective language, and organize it into the most attractive layout. First, let's take a look at each of these important elements individually.

Heading

The heading may seem to be a simple enough element in your resume, but be careful not to take it lightly. The heading should be placed at the top of your resume and should include your name, home address, and telephone numbers. If you can take calls at your current place of business, include your business number, since most employers will attempt to contact you during the business day. If this is not possible, or if you can afford it, purchase an answering machine that allows you to retrieve your messages while you are away from home. This way you can make sure you don't miss important phone calls. Always include your phone number on your resume. It is crucial that when prospective employers need to have immediate contact with you, they can.

Objective

When seeking a particular career path, it is important to list a job objective on your resume. This statement helps employers know the direction that you see yourself heading, so that they can determine whether your goals are in line with the position available. The objective is normally one sentence long and describes your employment goals clearly and concisely. See the sample resumes in this book for examples of objective statements.

The job objective will vary depending on the type of person you are, the field you are in, and the type of goals you have. It can be either specific or general, but it should always be to the point.

In some cases, this element is not necessary, but usually it is a good idea to include your objective. It gives your possible future employer an idea of where you are coming from and where you want to go.

The objective statement is better left out, however, if you are uncertain of the exact title of the job you seek. In such a case, the inclusion of an overly specific objective statement could result in your not being considered for a variety of acceptable positions; you should be sure to incorporate this information in your cover letter, instead.

Work Experience

This element is arguably the most important of them all. It will provide the central focus of your resume, so it is necessary that this section be as complete as possible. Only by examining your work experience in depth can you get to the heart of your accomplishments and present them in a way that demonstrates the strength of your qualifications. Of course, someone just out of school will have less work experience than someone who has been working for a number of years, but the amount of information isn't the most important thing—rather, how it is presented and how it highlights you as a person and as a worker will be what counts.

As you work on this section of your resume, be aware of the need for accuracy. You'll want to include all necessary information about each of your jobs, including job title, dates, employer, city, state, responsibilities, special projects, and accomplishments. Be sure to only list company accomplishments for which you were directly responsible. If you haven't participated in any special projects, that's all right—this area may not be relevant to certain jobs.

The most common way to list your work experience is in *reverse chronological order.* In other words, start with your most recent job and work your way backwards. This way your prospective employer sees your current (and often most important) job before seeing your past jobs. Your most recent position, if the most important, should also be the one that includes the most information, as compared to your previous positions. If you are just out of school, show your summer employment and part-time work, though in this case your education will most likely be more important than your work experience.

The following worksheets will help you gather information about your past jobs.

WORK EXPERIENCE
Job One:

Job Title _____

Dates _____

Employer _____

City, State _____

Major Duties _____

_____

_____

_____

_____

_____

_____

_____

Special Projects _____

_____

_____

_____

Accomplishments _____

_____

_____

_____

_____

_____

_____

_____

Job Two:

Job Title _____

Dates _____

Employer _____

City, State _____

Major Duties _____

_____

_____

_____

_____

_____

_____

Special Projects _____

_____

_____

_____

Accomplishments_____

_____

_____

_____

_____

_____

_____

_____

Job Three:

Job Title _____

Dates _____

Employer _____

City, State _____

Major Duties _____

_____

_____

_____

_____

_____

_____

_____

Special Projects _____

_____

_____

_____

Accomplishments_____

_____

_____

_____

_____

_____

_____

_____

_____

Job Four:

Job Title _____

Dates _____

Employer _____

City, State _____

Major Duties _____

_____

_____

_____

_____

_____

_____

_____

Special Projects _____

_____

_____

_____

Accomplishments_____

_____

_____

_____

_____

_____

_____

_____

Education

Education is the second most important element of a resume. Your educational background is often a deciding factor in an employer's decision to hire you. Be sure to stress your accomplishments in school with the same finesse that you stressed your accomplishments at work. If you are looking for your first job, your education will be your greatest asset, since your work experience will most likely be minimal. In this case, the education section becomes the most important. You will want to be sure to include any degrees or certificates you received, your major area of concentration, any honors, and any relevant activities. Again, be sure to list your most recent schooling first. If you have completed graduate-level work, begin with that and work in reverse chronological order through your undergraduate education. If you have completed an undergraduate degree, you may choose whether to list your high school experience or not. This should be done only if your high school grade-point average was well above average.

The following worksheets will help you gather information for this section of your resume. Also included are supplemental worksheets for honors and for activities. Sometimes honors and activities are listed in a section separate from education, most often near the end of the resume.

EDUCATION

School _____

Major or Area of Concentration _____

Degree _____

Date _____

School _____

Major or Area of Concentration _____

Degree _____

Date _____

Honors

Here, you should list any awards, honors, or memberships in honorary societies that you have received. Usually these are of an academic nature, but they can also be for special achievement in sports, clubs, or other school activities. Always be sure to include the name of the organization honoring you and the date(s) received. Use the worksheet below to help gather your honors information.

HONORS

Honor: _____

Awarding Organization: _____

Date(s): _____

Honor: _____

Awarding Organization: _____

Date(s): _____

Honor: _____

Awarding Organization: _____

Date(s): _____

Honor: _____

Awarding Organization: _____

Date(s): _____

Activities

You may have been active in different organizations or clubs during your years at school; often an employer will look at such involvement as evidence of initiative and dedication. Your ability to take an active role, and even a leadership role, in a group should be included on your resume. Use the worksheet provided to list your activities and accomplishments in this area. In general, you should exclude any organization the name of which indicates the race, creed, sex, age, marital status, color, or nation of origin of its members.

ACTIVITIES

Organization/Activity: _____

Accomplishments: _____

_____

_____

Organization/Activity: _____

Accomplishments: _____

_____

_____

Organization/Activity: _____

Accomplishments: _____

_____

_____

Organization/Activity: _____

Accomplishments: _____

_____

_____

As your work experience increases through the years, your school activities and honors will play less of a role in your resume, and eventually you will most likely only list your degree and any major honors you received. This is due to the fact that, as time goes by, your job performance becomes the most important element in your resume. Through time, your resume should change to reflect this.

Certificates and Licenses

The next potential element of your resume is certificates and licenses. You should list these if the job you are seeking requires them and you, of course, have acquired them. If you have applied for a license, but have not yet received it, use the phrase "application pending."

License requirements vary by state. If you have moved or you are planning to move to another state, be sure to check with the appropriate board or licensing agency in the state in which you are applying for work to be sure that you are aware of all licensing requirements.

Always be sure that all of the information you list is completely accurate. Locate copies of your licenses and certificates and check the exact date and name of the accrediting agency. Use the following worksheet to list your licenses and certificates.

CERTIFICATES AND LICENSES

Name of License: _____

Licensing Agency: _____

Date Issued: _____

Name of License: _____

Licensing Agency: _____

Date Issued: _____

Name of License: _____

Licensing Agency: _____

Date Issued: _____

Professional Memberships

Another potential element in your resume is a section listing professional memberships. Use this section to list involvement in professional associations, unions, and similar organizations. It is to your advantage to list any professional memberships that pertain to the job you are seeking. Be sure to include the dates of your involvement and whether you took part in any special activities or held any offices within the organization. Use the following worksheet to gather your information.

PROFESSIONAL MEMBERSHIPS

Name of Organization: _____

Offices Held: _____

Activities: _____

Date(s): _____

Name of Organization: _____

Offices Held: _____

Activities: _____

Date(s): _____

Name of Organization: _____

Offices Held: _____

Activities: _____

Date(s): _____

Name of Organization: _____

Offices Held: _____

Activities: _____

Date(s): _____

Special Skills

This section of your resume is set aside for mentioning any special abilities you have that could relate to the job you are seeking. This is the part of your resume where you have the opportunity to demonstrate certain talents and experiences that are not necessarily a part of your educational or work experience. Common examples include fluency in a foreign language, or knowledge of a particular computer application.

Special skills can encompass a wide range of your talents—remember to be sure that whatever skills you list relate to the type of work you are looking for.

Personal Information

Some people include "Personal" information on their resumes. This is not generally recommended, but you might wish to include it if you think that something in your personal life, such as a hobby or talent, has some bearing on the position you are seeking. This type of information is often referred to at the beginning of an interview, when it is used as an "ice breaker." Of course, personal information regarding age, marital status, race, religion, or sexual preference should never appear on any resume.

References

References are not usually listed on the resume, but a prospective employer needs to know that you have references who may be contacted if necessary. All that is necessary to include in your resume regarding references is a sentence at the bottom stating, "References are available upon request." If a prospective employer requests a list of references, be sure to have one ready. Also, check with whomever you list to see if it is all right for you to use them as a reference. Forewarn them that they may receive a call regarding a reference for you. This way they can be prepared to give you the best reference possible.

Chapter Two

WRITING YOUR RESUME

*N*ow that you have gathered together all of the information for each of the sections of your resume, it's time to write out each section in a way that will get the attention of whoever is reviewing it. The type of language you use in your resume will affect its success. You want to take the information you have gathered and translate it into a language that will cause a potential employer to sit up and take notice.

Resume writing is not like expository writing or creative writing. It embodies a functional, direct writing style and focuses on the use of action words. By using action words in your writing, you more effectively stress past accomplishments. Action words help demonstrate your initiative and highlight your talents. Always use verbs that show strength and reflect the qualities of a "doer." By using action words, you characterize yourself as a person who takes action, and this will impress potential employers.

The following is a list of verbs commonly used in resume writing. Use this list to choose the action words that can help your resume become a strong one:

administered	introduced
advised	invented
analyzed	maintained
arranged	managed
assembled	met with
assumed responsibility	motivated
billed	negotiated
built	operated
carried out	orchestrated
channeled	ordered
collected	organized
communicated	oversaw
compiled	performed
completed	planned
conducted	prepared
contacted	presented
contracted	produced
coordinated	programmed
counseled	published
created	purchased
cut	recommended
designed	recorded
determined	reduced
developed	referred
directed	represented
dispatched	researched
distributed	reviewed
documented	saved
edited	screened
established	served as
expanded	served on
functioned as	sold
gathered	suggested
handled	supervised
hired	taught
implemented	tested
improved	trained
inspected	typed
interviewed	wrote

Now take a look at the information you put down on the work experience worksheets. Take that information and rewrite it in paragraph form, using verbs to highlight your actions and accomplishments. Let's look at an example, remembering that what matters here is the writing style, and not the particular job responsibilities given in our sample.

WORK EXPERIENCE
Regional Sales Manager

Manager of sales representatives from seven states. Responsible for twelve food chain accounts in the East. In charge of directing the sales force in planned selling toward specific goals. Supervisor and trainer of new sales representatives. Consulting for customers in the areas of inventory management and quality control.

Special Projects: Coordinator and sponsor of annual food industry sales seminar.

Accomplishments: Monthly regional volume went up 25 percent during my tenure while, at the same time, a proper sales/cost ratio was maintained. Customer/company relations improved significantly.

Below is the rewritten version of this information, using action words. Notice how much stronger it sounds.

WORK EXPERIENCE
Regional Sales Manager

Managed sales representatives from seven states. Handled twelve food chain accounts in the eastern United States. Directed the sales force in planned selling towards specific goals. Supervised and trained new sales representatives. Consulted for customers in the areas of inventory management and quality control. Coordinated and sponsored the annual Food Industry Seminar. Increased monthly regional volume 25 percent and helped to improve customer/company relations during my tenure.

Another way of constructing the work experience section is by using actual job descriptions. Job descriptions are rarely written using the proper resume language, but they do include all the information necessary to create this section of your resume. Take the description of one of the jobs your are including on your resume (if you have access to it), and turn it into an action-oriented paragraph. Below is an example of a job description followed by a version of the same description written using action words. Again, pay attention to the style of writing, as the details of your own work experience will be unique.

PUBLIC ADMINISTRATOR I

Responsibilities: Coordinate and direct public services to meet the needs of the nation, state, or community. Analyze problems; work with special committees and public agencies; recommend solutions to governing bodies.

Aptitudes and Skills: Ability to relate to and communicate with people; solve complex problems through analysis; plan, organize, and implement policies and programs. Knowledge of political systems; financial management; personnel administration; program evaluation; organizational theory.

WORK EXPERIENCE
Public Administrator I

Wrote pamphlets and conducted discussion groups to inform citizens of legislative processes and consumer issues. Organized and supervised 25 interviewers. Trained interviewers in effective communication skills.

Now that you have learned how to word your resume, you are ready for the next step in your quest for a winning resume: assembly and layout.

Chapter Three

ASSEMBLY AND LAYOUT

*A*t this point, you've gathered all the necessary information for your resume, and you've rewritten it using the language necessary to impress potential employers. Your next step is to assemble these elements in a logical order and then to lay them out on the page neatly and attractively in order to achieve the desired effect: getting that interview.

Assembly

The order of the elements in a resume makes a difference in its overall effect. Obviously, you would not want to put your name and address in the middle of the resume or your special skills section at the top. You want to put the elements in an order that stresses your most important achievements, not the less pertinent information. For example, if you recently graduated from school and have no full-time work experience, you will want to list your education before you list any part-time jobs you may have held during school. On the other hand, if you have been gainfully employed for several years and currently hold an important position in your company, you will want to list your work experience ahead of your education, which has become less pertinent with time.

There are some elements that are always included in your resume and some that are optional. Following is a list of essential and optional elements:

Essential	*Optional*
Name	Job Objective
Address	Honors
Phone Number	Special Skills
Work Experience	Professional Memberships
Education	Activities
References Phrase	Certificates and Licenses
	Personal Information

Your choice of optional sections depends on your own background and employment needs. Always use information that will put you and your abilities in a favorable light. If your honors are impressive, then be sure to include them in your resume. If your activities in school demonstrate particular talents necessary for the job you are seeking, then allow space for a section on activities. Each resume is unique, just as each person is unique.

Types of Resumes

So far, our discussion about resumes has involved the most common type—the *reverse chronological* resume, in which your most recent job is listed first and so on. This is the type of resume usually preferred by human resources directors, and it is the one most frequently used. However, in some cases this style of presentation is not the most effective way to highlight your skills and accomplishments.

For someone reentering the work force after many years or someone looking to change career fields, the *functional resume* may work best. This type of resume focuses more on achievement and less on the sequence of your work history. In the functional resume, your experience is presented by what you have accomplished and the skills you have developed in your past work.

A functional resume can be assembled from the same information you collected for your chronological resume. The main difference lies in how you organize this information. Essentially, the work experience section becomes two sections, with your job duties and accomplishments comprising one section and your employer's name, city, state, your position, and the dates employed making up another section. The first section is placed near the top of the resume, just below the job objective section, and can be called *Accomplishments* or *Achievements*. The second section, containing the bare essentials of your employment history, should come after the accomplishments section and can be titled *Work Experience* or *Employment History*. The other sections of your resume remain the same. The work experience section is the only one affected in the functional resume. By placing the section that focuses on your achievements first, you thereby draw attention to these achievements. This puts less emphasis on who you worked for and more emphasis on what you did and what you are capable of doing.

For someone changing careers, emphasis on skills and achievements is essential. The identities of previous employers, which may be unrelated to one's new job field, need to be downplayed. The functional resume accomplishes this task. For someone reentering the work force after many years, a functional resume is the obvious choice. If you lack full-time work experience, you will need to draw attention away from this fact and instead focus on your skills and abilities gained possibly through volunteer activities or part-time work. Education may also play a more important role in this resume.

Which type of resume is right for you will depend on your own personal circumstances. It may be helpful to create a chronological *and* a functional resume and then compare the two to find out which is more suitable. The sample resumes found in this book include both chronological and functional resumes. Use these resumes as guides to help you decide on the content and appearance of your own resume.

Layout

Once you have decided which elements to include in your resume and you have arranged them in an order that makes sense and emphasizes your achievements and abilities, then it is time to work on the physical layout of your resume.

There is no single appropriate layout that applies to every resume, but there are a few basic rules to follow in putting your resume on paper:

1. Leave a comfortable margin on the sides, top, and bottom of the page (usually 1 to 1½ inches).

2. Use appropriate spacing between the sections (usually 2 to 3 line spaces are adequate).

3. Be consistent in the *type* of headings you use for the different sections of your resume. For example, if you capitalize the heading EMPLOYMENT HISTORY, don't use initial capitals and underlining for a heading of equal importance, such as <u>Education</u>.

4. Always try to fit your resume onto one page. If you are having trouble fitting all your information onto one page, perhaps you are trying to say too much. Try to edit out any repetitive or unnecessary information or possibly shorten descriptions of earlier jobs. Be ruthless. Maybe you've included too many optional sections.

CHRONOLOGICAL RESUME

ANGELA ROMANO

Address:

421 White Street
Buffalo, NY 14222
(716) 555-9587

PROFESSIONAL SUMMARY

Experienced counselor with special emphasis on substance abuse counseling

WORK EXPERIENCE

1993-Present	Counselor, Buffalo Mental Health Services, Buffalo, New York
1991-93	Counselor, Buffalo City Schools, Buffalo, New York
1990-91	Mental Health Assistant, Buffalo Mental Health Services (Part-time)

EDUCATION

B.S., Buffalo State College, 1991
    Major: Counseling
    Minor: Psychology

A.S., Erie Community College, 1989
    Curriculum: Mental Health Assistant: Alcohol Counseling

SPECIAL SKILLS/CERTIFICATIONS

Fully certified by State of New York through comprehensive examination process

Skilled in various counseling areas, with extensive experience in problems related to drug and alcohol abuse

Active speaker for youth organizations and civic groups

REFERENCES

Provided on request

FUNCTIONAL RESUME

Steven Ryder
8001 Dover Avenue
Indianapolis, IN 46202
(317) 555-7460

PROFESSIONAL EXPERIENCE

Eight years of experience in grant coordination and management including six years as Intergovernmental Grant Coordinator, Indiana State Budget Agency

JOB DUTIES

- Coordinated state's "Single Point of Contact" program in response to Executive Order 12372

- Reviewed state-level grant proposals submitted to Federal agencies

- Managed indirect cost recovery program

- Coordinated state approval process for proposals submitted by more than fifteen state agencies and departments

- Prepared summary reports of state-wide proposal development activity and funding results

- Assisted in development and refinement of policies and procedures regarding involvement of state agencies and departments in projects funded by Federal and private funds

EDUCATIONAL BACKGROUND

B.S., Indiana University, 1987
Major: Political Science

M.S., Indiana University, 1989
Major: Public Administration

REFERENCES

Available on request

Don't let the idea of having to tell every detail about your life get in the way of producing a resume that is simple and straightforward. The more compact your resume, the easier it will be to read and the better an impression it will make for you.

In some cases, the resume will not fit on a single page, even after extensive editing. In such cases, the resume should be printed on two pages so as not to compromise clarity or appearance. Each page of a two-page resume should be marked clearly with your name and the page number, e.g., "Judith Ramirez, page 1 of 2." The pages should then be stapled together.

Try experimenting with various layouts until you find one that looks good to you. Always show your final layout to other people and ask them what they like or dislike about it, and what impresses them most about your resume. Make sure that is what you want most to emphasize. If it isn't, you may want to consider making changes in your layout until the necessary information is emphasized. Use the sample resumes in this book to get some ideas for laying out your resume.

Putting Your Resume in Print

Your resume should be typed or printed on good quality 8½" × 11" bond paper. You want to make as good an impression as possible with your resume; therefore, quality paper is a necessity. If you have access to a word processor with a good printer, or know of someone who does, make use of it. Typewritten resumes should only be used when there are no other options available.

After you have produced a clean original, you will want to make duplicate copies of it. Usually a copy shop is your best bet for producing copies without smudges or streaks. Make sure you have the copy shop use quality bond paper for all copies of your resume. Ask for a sample copy before they run your entire order. After copies are made, check each copy for cleanliness and clarity.

Another more costly option is to have your resume typeset and printed by a printer. This will provide the most attractive resume of all. If you anticipate needing a lot of copies of your resume, the cost of having it typeset may be justified.

Proofreading

After you have finished typing the master copy of your resume and before you go to have it copied or printed, you must thoroughly check it for typing and spelling errors. Have several people read it over just in case you may have missed an error. Misspelled words and typing mistakes will not make a good impression on a prospective employer, as they are a bad reflection on your writing ability and your attention to detail. With thorough and conscientious proofreading, these mistakes can be avoided.

The following are some rules of capitalization and punctuation that may come in handy when proofreading your resume:

Rules of Capitalization

- Capitalize proper nouns, such as names of schools, colleges, and universities, names of companies, and brand names of products.

- Capitalize major words in the names and titles of books, tests, and articles that appear in the body of your resume.

- Capitalize words in major section headings of your resume.

- Do not capitalize words just because they seem important.

- When in doubt, consult a manual of style such as *Words Into Type* (Prentice-Hall), or *The Chicago Manual of Style* (The University of Chicago Press). Your local library can help you locate these and other reference books.

Rules of Punctuation

- Use a comma to separate words in a series.

- Use a semicolon to separate series of words that already include commas within the series.

- Use a semicolon to separate independent clauses that are not joined by a conjunction.

- Use a period to end a sentence.

- Use a colon to show that the examples or details that follow expand or amplify the preceding phrase.

- Avoid the use of dashes.

- Avoid the use of brackets.

- If you use any punctuation in an unusual way in your resume, be consistent in its use.

- Whenever you are uncertain, consult a style manual.

Chapter Four

THE COVER LETTER

*O*nce your resume has been assembled, laid out, and printed to your satisfaction, the next and final step before distribution is to write your cover letter. Though there may be instances where you deliver your resume in person, most often you will be sending it through the mail. Resumes sent through the mail always need an accompanying letter that briefly introduces you and your resume. The purpose of the cover letter is to get a potential employer to read your resume, just as the purpose of your resume is to get that same potential employer to call you for an interview.

Like your resume, your cover letter should be clean, neat, and direct. A cover letter usually includes the following information:

1. Your name and address (unless it already appears on your personal letterhead).

2. The date.

3. The name and address of the person and company to whom you are sending your resume.

4. The salutation ("Dear Mr." or "Dear Ms." followed by the person's last name, or "To Whom It May Concern" if you are answering a blind ad).

5. An opening paragraph explaining why you are writing (in response to an ad, the result of a previous meeting, at the suggestion of someone you both know) and indicating that you are interested in whatever job is being offered.

6. One or two more paragraphs that tell why you want to work for the company and what qualifications and experience you can bring to that company.

7. A final paragraph that closes the letter and requests that you be contacted for an interview. You may mention here that your references are available upon request.

8. The closing ("Sincerely," or "Yours Truly," followed by your signature with your name typed under it).

Your cover letter, including all of the information above, should be no more than one page in length. The language used should be polite, businesslike, and to the point. Do not attempt to tell your life story in the cover letter. A long and cluttered letter will only serve to put off the reader. Remember, you only need to mention a few of your accomplishments and skills in the cover letter. The rest of your information is in your resume. Each and every achievement should not be mentioned twice. If your cover letter is a success, your resume will be read and all pertinent information reviewed by your prospective employer.

Producing the Cover Letter

Cover letters should always be typed individually, since they are always written to particular individuals and companies. Never use a form letter for your cover letter. Cover letters cannot be copied or reproduced like resumes. Each one should be as personal as possible. Of course, once you have written and rewritten your first cover letter to the point where you are satisfied with it, you certainly can use similar wording in subsequent letters.

After you have typed your cover letter on quality bond paper, be sure to proofread it as thoroughly as you did your resume. Again, spelling errors are a sure sign of carelessness, and you don't want that to be a part of your first impression on a prospective employer. Make sure to handle the letter and resume carefully to avoid any smudges, and then mail both your cover letter and resume in an appropriate sized envelope. Be sure to keep an accurate record of all the resumes you send out and the results of each mailing, either in a separate notebook or on individual 3 × 5" index cards.

Numerous sample cover letters appear at the end of the book. Use them as models for your own cover letter or to get an idea of how cover letters are put together. Remember, every one is unique and depends on the particular circumstances of the individual writing it and the job for which he or she is applying.

Now the job of writing your resume and cover letter is complete. About a week after mailing resumes and cover letters to potential employers, you will want to contact them by telephone. Confirm that your resume arrived, and ask whether an interview might be possible. Getting your foot in the door during this call is half the battle of a job search, and a strong resume and cover letter will help you immeasurably.

Chapter Five

SAMPLE RESUMES

This chapter contains dozens of sample resumes for people pursuing a wide variety of jobs and careers.

There are many different styles of resumes in terms of graphic layout and presentation of information. These samples also represent people with varying amounts of education and experience. Use these samples to model your own resume after. Choose one resume, or borrow elements from several different resumes to help you construct your own.

DON P. HARRELL
3229 Roanoke Street
Nashville, TN 37219
(617) 555-3215

Career Objective

POSITION IN ENVIRONMENTAL HEALTH OR RELATED AREA

Occupational Accomplishments

Served as an environmental health inspector, employed by the state of Tennessee, 1991-95

- Conducted on-site inspections

- Completed reports based on field work

- Advised staff of various facilities on appropriate measures for achieving optimum environmental cleanliness and health

- Developed improved records management system for maintaining regional inspection records

- Earned excellent performance evaluations and earned two citations for excellence

Educational Background

B.S. East Tennessee State University, 1991

Major: Environmental Health

Minor: Biology

References

Complete reference information available

Michael Q. Davis
11-C Sterling Lane Townhouses
Gloucester, MA 01930
(617) 555-2305 (voice)
(617) 555-6506 (fax)

PROFESSIONAL EXPERIENCE

Current Position

Staff Meteorologist, National Oceanic and Atmospheric
Administration, Gloucester, Massachusetts

In this position, I conduct meteorological research for use
in various scientific studies and for use by government
agencies.

Previous Experience

Eleven years of experience with the United States Navy
as a Meteorology/Oceanography Limited Duty Officer.

In this role, I provided meteorological and oceanographic
support for naval operations.

EDUCATION

A.A.S., Jefferson Community College, Louisville, Kentucky

B.S., University of Kentucky, Lexington, Kentucky
    Major: Geology
    Minor: Physics

M.S., Massachusetts Institute of Technology, Cambridge,
Massachusetts
    Major: Meteorology
    Thesis: "Effect of West African Rainfall on Western
             Atlantic Hurricane Generation"

Various special courses also completed through U.S. Navy
training programs

REFERENCES

Available on request

Leigh Van Sise
P.O. Box 778
Carol Stream, IL 60118
(617) 555-9811

PROFESSIONAL EXPERIENCE

Assessor, Grundy County, Illinois, 1989-96

--Supervised all activities of assessor's office in valuing and clarifying county real estate for tax purposes

--Determined appropriate market value of property as mandated by state and county laws

--Coordinated appraisal and reappraisal process

--Communicated assessment methods to the public and explained appeal procedures

--Supervised staff of three clerical personnel

Deputy Assessor, Grundy County, Illinois, 1985-89

--Performed a variety of duties related to the assessment process

Realtor, Thomas Realty, Carol Stream, Illinois, 1978-85

--Served as a key member of a full-service real estate agency

EDUCATION

Bachelor of Science, Wheaton College

Major: Real Estate

Grade Point Average: 3.66

REFERENCES

Available on request

Resume of:
Hannah Sexton-Boyd
11 Bayview Drive
Apartment 22H
Honolulu, Hawaii 96825
(808) 555-3640

WORK EXPERIENCE

1994-Present   Secretary Senior
                Hawaii Department of Education
                Honolulu, Hawaii

1991-1994   Clerk-Typist
                Hawaii Department of Education

EDUCATIONAL BACKGROUND

A.S. in Secretarial Science
University of Hawaii, Honolulu Community College

Also completed continuing education seminars in WordPerfect,
The Effective Assistant, Time Management and other topics

SKILLS/COMPETENCIES

Excellent word processing skills

Highly proficient in use of oral dictation systems

Outstanding communication skills (both written and oral)

Well-organized and efficient in file management and other
information management

Task-oriented, productive and reliable

Named "Outstanding Classified Staff" employee, Hawaii
Department of Education, 1995

REFERENCES

Provided on request

TINA ALLISON
P.O. Box 728
Milwaukee, WI 53217
(414) 555-3202

SUMMARY OF QUALIFICATIONS

Competent, highly experienced graphic artist. Skilled in developing various types of graphic illustrations for use in a wide range of applications.

AREAS OF EXPERTISE

*Pen and ink drawings

*Computer-generated graphics

*Photography (both full-color and black-and-white)

*Layout and design

*Illustrations of all types

*Production of brochures, flyers, catalogs, posters

*Logo and letterhead design

*Cooperative ventures involving writer-artist collaboration

*Computer applications in layout, design and graphic production

EMPLOYMENT HISTORY

1993-Present   Wisconsin Department of Executive Management

Position: Graphic Artist

Duties: Performing a wide range of duties as part of public information department for governor's office and other offices within the executive branch.

Allison, 1 of 2

Allison, 2 of 2

1991-93   Wisconsin Department of Personnel and
               Training

Position: Graphic Technician

Duties: Provided full spectrum of graphic services in
developing newsletters, manuals and other publications.

1990-91   Wisconsin Department of Personnel and
               Training

Position: Graphics Intern

Duties: Assisted graphic artists in various design and
illustration projects

EDUCATION

A.A.S, Milwaukee Area Technical College, 1991.
Course of study included twenty-four semester hours in
graphic communications

Also completed several courses/seminars in Corel Draw,
Ventura and other topics

SAMPLE WORK

Portfolio or samples of work provided on request

REFERENCES

Available on request

Richard E. Weiss
890 Bagging Plant Road
Albany, NY 12243
(518) 555-6789

WORK EXPERIENCE

1991-Present
Public Works Inspector
New York Department of Highways
Albany, New York

1988-91
Construction Inspector
Pennsylvania Highway Department
Scranton, Pennsylvania

1984-88
Project Supervisor
Allen and Smith Construction, Inc.
Scranton, Pennsylvania

1982-84
Construction Engineer
Allen and Smith Construction
Scranton, Pennsylvania

EDUCATIONAL BACKGROUND

B.S., Clarion State University, 1982
Major: Civil Engineering
Minor: Architectural Drafting

JOB SKILLS

Skilled in various aspects of construction inspection with
specialty in public works. Experienced in construction and
inspection of bridges, tunnels and highways. Highly
knowledgeable in state and federal codes. Effective in
written and oral communications.

MEMBERSHIPS

American Society of Civil Engineers
Building Officials and Code Administrations International

REFERENCES provided on request

Douglas A. Cozzins   113 Speer Street, North
                                            Kansas City, MO 64153
                                            (816) 555-5018

OBJECTIVE: A challenging position as a paralegal

RELEVANT SKILLS AND EXPERIENCE

> Experienced in various aspects of paralegal work with
> emphasis on a nonprofit, government setting

> Skilled in legal research techniques

> Experienced in evidence collection and analysis

> Skilled in preparing a wide range of informational
> materials for use by attorneys and management staff

> Adept at computer applications in legal research,
> analysis and record-keeping

WORK HISTORY

1992-Present

> Paralegal
> Missouri Department of Human Service
> Kansas City, Missouri

1989-92

> Paralegal
> U.S. Department of Education
> Region VII Office
> Kansas City, Missouri

EDUCATION

A.S. in Paralegal Studies
Johnson County Community College
Overland Park, Kansas, 1989

REFERENCES ON REQUEST

MICHELLE NGUYEN
441 Golden Palace Drive
P.O. Box 1124
San Francisco, CA 94102
(415) 555-7570

CAREER OBJECTIVE: A position in court reporting or related area

EXPERIENCE

- Court Reporter, Ninth District Federal Court, San Francisco, California, 1992-Present

- Court Reporter, California Court System, Oakland, California, 1988-92

- Free-lance caption writer and word processing specialist, 1986-88

PROFESSIONAL SKILLS/CAPABILITIES

- Accomplished court reporter with proven speed and reliability. Consistent recording speed of more than 225 words per minute.

- Skilled in use of both computer transcription systems and mechanical stenotype machines. Also skilled in manual transcription.

- Reliable employee with no absences over the past five years

- Recipient of award of excellence from California Shorthand Reporters Association

EDUCATIONAL BACKGROUND

A.A.S., Mission College, Santa Clara, California

Major: Court Reporting

Also completed several continuing education courses sponsored by professional organizations

Page 1 of 2

Nguyen, Page 2 of 2

MEMBERSHIPS

California Court Reporters Association

National Shorthand Reporters Association

COMMUNITY INVOLVEMENT

Active volunteer in several community organizations, including United Way and Sierra Club

REFERENCES AVAILABLE ON REQUEST

Marcie Copenhaver
1322 Anderson Drive
Dallas, Texas 75202
(214) 555-9634

Professional Experience

1992-Present
    Assistant Director, Region VI
    U.S. Department of Education
    Dallas, Texas

1990-92
    Coordinator of Special Projects
    U.S. Department of Education, Region VI

1988-90
    Assistant Program Director, Vocational and Technical
        Education
    Texas Department of Education
    Austin, Texas

1979-88
    Associate Professor of Education
    University of Texas at Austin

Educational Background

B.A., University of Oklahoma
    Major: Education
    Minor: Statistics

M.S., Oklahoma State University
    Major: Vocational and Technical Education

Ph.D., Oklahoma State University
    Major area: Adult and Continuing Education

Publications

Over 20 articles in professional journals; complete list
available

References

Available on request

Steven Ryder
8001 Dover Avenue
Indianapolis, IN 46202
(317) 555-7460

PROFESSIONAL EXPERIENCE

Eight years of experience in grant coordination and management including six years as Intergovernmental Grant Coordinator, Indiana State Budget Agency

JOB DUTIES

- Coordinated state's "Single Point of Contact" program in response to Executive Order 12372

- Reviewed state-level grant proposals submitted to Federal agencies

- Managed indirect cost recovery program

- Coordinated state approval process for proposals submitted by more than fifteen state agencies and departments

- Prepared summary reports of state-wide proposal development activity and funding results

- Assisted in development and refinement of policies and procedures regarding involvement of state agencies and departments in projects funded by Federal and private funds

EDUCATIONAL BACKGROUND

B.S., Indiana University, 1987
Major: Political Science

M.S., Indiana University, 1989
Major: Public Administration

REFERENCES

Available on request

EMILY WYNN
212 Afton Place
Albany, New York 12201
(518) 555-3238

Objective

A challenging position in installation, service and repair of electronic equipment

Experience

- Have served as an electronics technician for the Federal Bureau of Investigation, 1992-present. Specialty is service and repair of various types of electronic equipment.

- Experienced in all aspects of maintaining electronic equipment and components

- Installed communications equipment, forensics testing equipment, computers, office equipment and other electronic systems and devices

- Identified equipment malfunctions and instituted appropriate replacement/repair options

- Advised staff on proper use and care of electronic equipment as well as equipment selection

Education

Completed two-year, associate degree program in electronics technology at Suffolk County Community College, Selden, New York, 1992. Electronics and related courses completed included:

--Technical Mathematics I and II
--Technical Physics I and II
--DC Circuits
--Digital Electronics
--Electronics I, II and III
--Microprocessors I and II
--Industrial Electronics

References

Provided on request

RICK SCOTT

6 Pine Tree Place
Wellington Estates
100 Northside Avenue
Lakewood, CO 80225
(303) 555-4259

EDUCATIONAL BACKGROUND

Two years of course work in forestry, University of Colorado

Additional training through completion of continuing education courses and seminars

Graduate, Eisenhower High School, Lakewood, Colorado

WORK EXPERIENCE

1989-96   Fish and Game Warden
            Colorado Department of Natural Resources

1986-89   Assistant Manager
            Rich Creek Game Preserve
            Grand Junction, Colorado

1985-86   Sales Clerk
            Lakewood Hardware
            Lakewood, Colorado

SPECIAL SKILLS

Experienced in all legal and administrative aspects of fish and game management

Experienced hunting guide

Fluent in Spanish

REFERENCES

Available on request

SUSAN A. WOO
825 Riverdale Avenue, Fairfax, VA 22033
(703) 555-8057

OBJECTIVE

To obtain challenging employment in a computer support
position

RELATED EXPERIENCE AND SKILLS

- Skilled in various aspects of computer programming
  and applications including program development and
  testing

- Highly experienced in all aspects of systems analysis

- Experienced in using a variety of computer languages
  including BASIC, C, COBOL, Assembler, RPG and
  FORTRAN

- Competent in problem-solving and applying advanced
  programming techniques

- Experienced in applying a teamwork approach to
  program development

EMPLOYMENT BACKGROUND

Programmer/Analyst, United States Department of Education,
    1990-present.

Duties: In this position, I am responsible for a wide
variety of duties involving both systems analysis and
programming. Major portion of work supports educational
research within the Office of Educational Research and
Improvement.

Sales Associate, Software Connections, Fairfax, Virginia,
    1989-90.

Duties: Advised customers and potential customers regarding
selection and use of computer software.

Woo, 1 of 2

EDUCATION

Bachelor of Science, Virginia Commonwealth University, 1989.
    Major: Computer Science
    Honors: Dean's List six semesters, Alpha Kappa Pi Honor
    Society, cum laude graduate

Associate in Science, Northern Virginia Community College,
    1985-86. Completed thirty credit hours of general
    studies before transferring. 3.85 grade point average.

MEMBERSHIPS

Member, Data Processing Management Association

Program Chairperson, Women in Computing (Washington, DC
Chapter)

REFERENCES

Complete reference information provided on request

NORA L. KLEIN
1426 Wilson Avenue
Hagerstown, MD 21741
Phone (301) 555-4865
Fax (301) 555-5990

PROFESSIONAL OBJECTIVE

To obtain a rewarding position in financial management or accounting

EMPLOYMENT EXPERIENCE

1991-Present   Accountant, Division of Procurement, National
                Institute of Health, Rockville, Maryland.

Performed wide range of accounting tasks. Specialized in
cost accounting, but also performed some internal auditing
functions. Served with high degree of reliability and
accuracy. Earned outstanding performance evaluations.
Developed solid track record based on thoroughness and
attention to detail. As a staff member in the Division of
Procurement, job tasks included the following:

* Performed a full array of standard accounting tasks

* Prepared budget documents

* Assisted in monitoring and reviewing equipment and
     supply expenditures

* Using both computers and traditional accounting
     methods, analyzed, computed and recorded financial
     transactions

* Completed various financial reports both
     independently and as a member of accounting
     team

1990-91   Fiscal Technician, HealthSafe Inc.,
           College Park, Maryland.

On a part-time basis (15 hours per week), provided basic
fiscal management services as assistant to chief accountant

page 1 of 2

Klein   Page 2

for firm specializing in sales of emergency health care equipment. Served in this capacity while completing senior year of college.

EDUCATION

Bachelor of Science Degree, University of Maryland, College Park, MD, 1991. Major: accounting. Minor: business management. Completed over 35 credit hours in accounting courses. Maintained 3.3 overall grade point average. Member, Accounting Club and Alpha Epsilon Business Honor Society.

Associate Degree, Hagerstown Community College, Hagerstown, MD, 1989. Completed 64 credit hours in business and general studies classes.

COMMUNITY SERVICE

Food bank volunteer
Member, Hagerstown Jaycees

REFERENCES
AVAILABLE
ON REQUEST

Joyce Taylor-Hall
17-B Lewis Townhomes
1118 South Maple Street
Herndon, VA 22071
(703) 555-1135

PROFESSIONAL EXPERIENCE

1994-Present   Contracting Officer
                  Materials Management Service
                  U.S. Interior Department
                  Herndon, Virginia

1991-94   Contract Specialist
                  Pittsburgh Energy Technology Center
                  U.S. Department of Energy
                  Pittsburgh, Pennsylvania

1990-91   Contract Technician
                  U.S. Department of Energy
                  Pittsburgh, Pennsylvania

1988-90   Accounting Clerk
                  Three Rivers Energy Systems
                  Pittsburgh, Pennsylvania

EDUCATIONAL BACKGROUND

A.S., Community College of Allegheny County, 1990
Major: Business
G.P.A.: 3.71

B.A. in progress, Shepherd College, Shepherdstown, West
Virginia (eighteen credit hours remaining to complete
Regents Bachelor of Arts Degree)

OFFICE SKILLS

--Skilled in fundamental accounting skills
--Experienced in using various types of office equipment
--Computer-literate

REFERENCES

Provided on request

Michelle L. Kwan
2958 Parkview Place   · Washington, DC 20036 · (202) 555-4549

Summary Resume

Education

Master of Arts, George Mason University, 1995
        Major: Asian Studies

Bachelor of Arts, George Mason University, 1990
        Major: History
        Minor: Political Science

Professional Experience

Foreign Affairs Analyst, U.S. State Department, 1990-94

Student Intern, U.S. State Department, 1993

Specialty: East Asian Affairs

Duties: Performed a wide variety of duties in compiling and analyzing information about East Asian affairs. Reviewed written documents, wrote summary reports, and served as junior member of policy advising team. Assisted in developing planning reports for review by senior managers. Earned excellent performance evaluations. Received citation for developing plan for enhanced storage of key records through micrographic reproduction. Reason for leaving: to complete graduate studies.

Special Skills and Interests

Fluent in Korean language. Highly interested in international affairs. Excellent skills in written and oral communication. Skilled in use of computers. Willing to travel.

References

Available on request.

THOMAS RYAN
2249 Carolina Avenue
Atlanta, GA 30341
(404) 555-2128 (voice)
(404) 555-5578 (fax)

Career Goal   A POSITION TAKING ADVANTAGE OF MY
BACKGROUND AND EXPERIENCE IN STATISTICS

**Achievements &
Experience**

Six years of service as a staff statistician specializing in
biostatistics, including the following duties:

- Performed a wide variety of duties related to
statistical analysis of human disease data.

- Served as an integral part of a four-person team
specializing in biostatistics.

- Analyzed annual data on disease incidences and
patterns.

- Assisted in development of cumulative reports for
release to the medical community and the public.

- Utilized and adapted computer software for
statistical analysis.

- Developed and refined new techniques for data
collection.

- Performed calculations and interpreted data in
verbal form.

- Received excellent performance ratings.

page 1 of 2

Ryan, Page 2

Work History

| 1989-Present | Staff Statistician, Centers for Disease Control and Prevention, Atlanta, GA. |
| 1988-89 | Intern, Department of Public Statistics, Georgia Department of Health, Atlanta |

Education

Bachelor of Science, Clemson University, Clemson, South Carolina, 1989.
Major: Statistics
Minor: Mathematics
G.P.A. : 3.9 in major, 3.5 overall

Courses completed included:

Applied Linear Regression
Analysis of Variance and Experimental Design
Probability and Mathematical Statistics (I and II)
Applied Nonparametric Statistics
Survey Sampling Methods
Statistical Quality Control
Stochastic Processes
Selected Topics in Statistics

References

Will be provided on request

GREGORY SMITH
Public Information Specialist

SUMMARY OF QUALIFICATIONS

Highly competent, experienced public information professional. Adept at various types of writing including feature articles, news releases, newsletters, annual reports, print ads and other material. Also skilled in use of desktop publishing software.

ACHIEVEMENTS

*Wrote award-winning series of feature articles highlighting volunteer efforts of Department of Commerce staff members

*Designed and wrote highly successful newsletter targeted to small businesses

*Completed an average of more than 500 news releases annually while carrying heavy workload with responsibility for a wide range of writing projects

*Cited as "Outstanding Young Talent" by Public Relations Society of America

WORK HISTORY

1990-96   Public Information Specialist, U.S. Department of Commerce, Washington, DC

Duties: Completed wide range of tasks in public information and public relations. Wrote news releases and worked with media representatives for appropriate placement. Designed newsletters and wrote copy. Wrote feature articles. Developed reports, brochures and other publications.

page 1 of 2

Smith/Page 2

1988-90   Publications Writer, George Washington University,
                   Washington, DC.

Duties: Developed publications for use by the Office of Institutional
Advancement including brochures for fund raising campaigns and articles for
alumni magazine.

EDUCATION

B.S., George Washington University, 1988.
        Major: Journalism
        Minor: Public/Community Relations
        G.P.A.: 3.9 in major; 3.5 overall

MEMBERSHIPS

Member, Public Relations Society of America

Member, Public Relations Society of Virginia and D.C.

REFERENCES

Available on request

323 Landview Place
Washington, DC 20002
(202) 555-8910

JUDY ANDERSON
333 St. Albans Drive, Raleigh, NC 27695
(919) 555-2636

PROFESSIONAL EXPERIENCE

1993-Present   Associate Network Director, National
                Institute of Environmental Health Sciences,
                Research Triangle Park, North Carolina

                Currently manage day to day operation of
                agency's computer network

                Developed data base and support systems

                Responsible for coordinating equipment
                acquisition, installation and maintenance

                Responsible for coordinating software
                acquisition and integration

                Responsible for training users and
                coordinating external training efforts

                Developed and implemented policies and
                procedures regarding network use

1991-93   Network Technician, National Institute of
                Environmental Health Sciences.

                Performed network management responsibilities
                under direction of network director.

SPECIAL SKILLS

- Highly skilled in all aspects of developing and
  coordinating a local area network

- Knowledgeable of wide area networks and other
  networking arrangements

- Up-to-date in hardware developments

                                        page 1 of 2

- Skilled in using various software packages

- Flexible and persistent in trouble-shooting, problem-solving and continuous improvement efforts

EDUCATION

B.S., University of North Carolina at Chapel Hill
Major: Mathematical Sciences

M.S. in progress (part-time), North Carolina State
University

REFERENCES

Available on request

David Goldstein, Jr.   411 South Mason Street
                                        Washington, DC 20002
                                        (202) 555-3290

OBJECTIVE: A position in forensic science or related area

RELEVANT SKILLS AND EXPERIENCE

> Experienced in various aspects of crime scene technology

> Skilled in sketching, diagramming and using casting materials

> Experienced in fingerprint classification and identification and latent techniques, drug identification, and hair and fiber evidence

> Skilled in thin-layer chromatographic methods

> Experienced in arson materials examination

WORK HISTORY

1992-Present

> Evidence Technician, Federal Bureau of Investigation, Washington, DC

EDUCATION

A.S. in Forensic Science
Northern Virginia Community College
Arlington, Virginia

Completed several FBI training courses

REFERENCES ON REQUEST

Manuel Hernandez
5466 Dunlap Avenue
Charlotte, NC 28244
(704) 555-3227

Objective

A position as an air traffic controller or a related position in aviation operation or management

Professional Experience

Eight years of experience as an air traffic controller. Currently employed through Federal Aviation Administration at Charlotte International Airport in Charlotte, North Carolina.

Experienced in providing both radar and non-radar air traffic control services

Skilled in Visual Flight Rules (VFR), Special Visual Flight Rules (SVFR) and Instrument Fight Rules (IFR)

Adept at teamwork and safe flight control practices

Fully qualified in all aspects of job with high marks on job performance examinations

Education

B.S., Stockton State College, 1988

Graduate, FAA Academy, Oklahoma City, Oklahoma, 1987

Successfully completed training and licensing as private pilot (small aircraft)

References

References and additional background information available on request.

MARY ANNE LIPINSKI
Route 2, Box 332
Pierre, South Dakota 57501
(605) 555-9811

OBJECTIVE

A rewarding position involving installation or repair of electronic equipment

CAREER BACKGROUND

Nine years of excellent service maintaining radar and other electronic equipment as a civilian employee of the U.S. Department of Defense

Installed and repaired electronic equipment at missile installations and other locations

Diagnosed malfunctions of electronic systems and components

Installed new electronic equipment and inspected and tested existing equipment

SPECIAL SKILLS

Highly skilled in using a variety of tools, testing devices and other equipment

Adept at trouble-shooting and creative approaches to systems repair

Flexible in working with different types of electronic equipment

EDUCATION

Diploma in Electronics Technology, Western Technical Institute, 1987

Additional training through Department of Defense continuing education classes

REFERENCES WILL BE PROVIDED ON REQUEST

Ann Rockland
1210 Eleventh Street
Salt Lake City, UT 84111
(801) 555-6461

Objective

A responsible position in child care or pre-school education

Professional Background

- Three years of experience as an assistant teacher in a Federally funded (Head Start) child care center

- Appropriately trained in providing for the care, health and safety of young children

- Skilled at helping children develop key socialization skills

- Proficient at communicating with young children

- Skilled in parent relations

- Experienced in helping children develop language and perceptional skills

- Creative and flexible in designing and coordinating recreational activities

- Certified in first aid

Education

Certificate in Early Childhood Development
Salt Lake Community College, 1993

Diploma, Robert Fleming High School, 1992

References

Available on request

ALISA F. RICHARDS
212 Laidley Avenue
Institute, West Virginia 25112
(304) 555-4341

CAREER OBJECTIVE

Responsible position in payroll or related business operations

Work Experience

West Virginia Department of Highways, 1989-Present.
Position: Payroll Specialist

Job tasks have included:

- Prepared payroll checks
- Maintained payroll support data
- Prepared travel documentation and issued reimbursement
- Assisted in implementing new computer payroll system
- Processed and documented various financial transactions

Education

Associate Degree, West Virginia State College, 1989
Major: Business Administration

Currently enrolled as a part-time student, pursuing a bachelor's degree in business administration at West Virginia State College

Memberships

Member, Mountain State Purchasing and Payroll Association

Member, Kanawha Valley Business Women's Association (currently vice president and program officer)

References

Complete reference information available on request

MARK A. BURNS
Apartment 24-C
Alpine Estates
Alexandria, VA 22314
(703) 555-3618

OBJECTIVE: A rewarding position in the management of human resources

PROFESSIONAL BACKGROUND

United States Department of Commerce, Washington, DC, 1989-Present

Positions:
Senior Personnel Specialist (1993-96)
Personnel Assistant (1989-93)

Duties:

▪Coordinated various aspects of hiring process for new personnel
▪Performed employee counseling services
▪Advised Department of Commerce personnel regarding various regulations
        and personnel procedures
▪Assisted in administering employee benefit programs
▪Maintained individual employment records
▪Assisted in planning and managing departmental budget
▪Performed a wide range of duties in human resources administration
▪Supervised a staff of 5 in providing basic personnel services as a part of larger
personnel unit

EDUCATION

Associate in Science, Northern Virginia Community College, Arlington, VA 1989
Major: Management
Grade point average: 3.75

Additional training completed 1990-present through non-credit continuing
education seminars and completion of 12 semester hours in personnel
administration at George Mason University

REFERENCES AVAILABLE ON REQUEST

CHARLES S. MALONE
33 Old South High Street · Bowling Green, KY 42101 · (502) 555-3619

RESUME

OBJECTIVE:

Private sector employment in mailroom management, general management or other area.

ACHIEVEMENTS:

Have served in progressively responsible positions with U.S. Postal Service. Named regional "Manager of the Year," 1994. Earned outstanding performance evaluations. Implemented quality circles and other management innovations.

WORK HISTORY:

1991-Present	Postmaster, East Bowling Green District, U.S. Postal Service, Bowling Green, Kentucky
1987-1991	Assistant Postmaster, East Bowling Green District, U.S. Postal Service
1983-1987	Mail Handler, East Bowling Green Office U.S. Postal Service
1980-1983	Postal Carrier, West Bowling Green District, U.S. Postal Service, Bowling Green, Kentucky
1978-1980	Stock Handler, Wilson Lumber, Bowling Green, Kentucky

EXPERIENCE:

Highly experienced in a broad range of management duties, including personnel

Page 1 of 2

Malone, Page 2

supervision, facilities management and public relations. Proven, effective manager with strong track record of efficient administrative leadership

EDUCATION:

B.S. Western Kentucky University, 1980

Major: History

Minor: Economics

Completed several master's level courses in personnel management and general management. Also completed non-credit training seminars on time management, dealing with difficult employees, public relations and other topics.

REFERENCES:

Available on request

MARY K. SMITH   1322 Twentieth Street, NW
                                   Apartment 21A
                                   Washington, DC 20036
                                   (202) 555-3141

CAREER OBJECTIVE: Responsible position requiring fluency in Spanish

EXPERIENCE

    1992-Present   U.S. Justice Department, Immigration and
                                   Naturalization Service, Washington, DC

    Position: Translator

    Duties: Have provided a wide range of translating duties,
                                   both oral and written. Assisted case workers and
                                   managers in communicating with applicants for
                                   naturalization. Translated documents from Spanish
                                   to English. Provided support services for
                                   Adjudication Unit.

EDUCATION

B.A. James Madison University, Harrisonburg, VA
Major: Spanish
Minor: Teacher Education
Honors: President of Spanish Club; Dean's List six semesters, <u>cum laude</u>
        graduate
Studied one semester at University of Madrid, Spain through Madison Scholars
        Exchange Program

SPECIAL SKILLS/KNOWLEDGE

Fluent in Spanish
Working knowledge of Italian, Portuguese, French
Highly skilled in oral and written communications

REFERENCES AVAILABLE ON REQUEST

LIONEL P. BURKES
118 S. Adams Street ＊Miami, FL 33126 ＊(305) 555-8785

EMPLOYMENT OBJECTIVE

To obtain a position involving social work or social services

CAREER HISTORY

Eight years of outstanding service as a social worker, specializing in case work related to the elderly. Earned excellent performance evaluations.

Work history has included part-time employment in the private sector as well as full-time work for the Dade County Social Services.

Desire to relocate to more rural area.

WORK BACKGROUND

Interviewed clients and identified problems to be addressed through health care and other county resources

Conducted group sessions

Developed and maintained case files

Completed reports and other documentation

Coordinated referrals related to seniors

EDUCATION

B.S. in Social Work, University of Georgia, 1987

REFERENCES WILL BE PROVIDED ON REQUEST

LAURA CHANDLER
2322 Holton Avenue
P.O. Box 11245
Alexandria, VA 22313
(703) 555-8537

Professional History

1992-Present	Program Officer, U.S. Department of Education, Washington, DC
Assignment:	Fund for the Improvement of Postsecondary Education (FIPSE)
Duties:	Responsible for coordinating and providing oversight for more than 100 multi-year grants awarded to colleges and universities throughout the United States. Routine tasks included monitoring progress of individual projects, reviewing evaluation reports, advising project directors on Federal regulations, assisting in problem resolution and developing content for RFP's (requests for proposals).
1981-92	Framington State College, Framington, MA
Assignments:	Associate Dean of Instruction, 1988-92 Associate Professor of History, 1986-88 Assistant Professor of History, 1981-86
Duties:	Broad variety of academic duties ranging from teaching history to assisting in managing the college's overall instructional program. Coordinated the college's academic advising program. Wrote numerous successful grant proposals and supervised several externally funded projects. Served as peer reviewer for U.S. Department of Education grant competitions.

Page 1 of 2

Chandler, 2

Education

Ph. D. in history, University of Massachusetts, 1981
Dissertation: <u>Moral Philosophy and the Abolitionist Movement, 1845-1861</u>
Honors: Graduate teaching assistant; recipient of departmental award for excellence in historical research

M.A. in history, Northeastern University, 1978
Honors: Graduate fellowship; member of Graduate Student Council

B.A., North Adams State College, 1976
Major: History
Minor: Political Science
<u>Summa cum laude</u> graduate

Memberships and Publications

Member, American Historical Association

Member, Alpha Kappa Episilon Honor Society

Publications in several educational and historical journals; complete list available on request

References

Available on request

Jessica P. Adams
34330 College Avenue
Little Rock, AR 72203
(501) 555-8901

CAREER OBJECTIVE

To obtain a position taking advantage of my skills as a highly trained and experienced home economist

RELATED EXPERIENCE

- Experienced in researching family buying and spending patterns

- Skilled in developing family budget guides

- Experienced in writing and lecturing on family living topics

- Highly skilled in research techniques, use of computers, and development of reports and publications

WORK BACKGROUND

Home Economist, Arkansas Department of Agriculture, 1992-Present.

Home Economics Teacher, Larchmont High School, 1988-92

EDUCATION

B.S., Arkansas State University, 1988

M.S., University of Tulsa, 1991.

Have completed over 40 semester hours and more than 30 graduate hours in home economics

REFERENCES PROVIDED ON REQUEST

JERRIE P. SPANGLER
14-B Red Maple Village
Laramie, WY 82071
(307) 555-3541

WORK EXPERIENCE

<u>1990-Present</u>
Fiscal Technician I (Buyer), Wyoming Department of
Corrections, Laramie, Wyoming

<u>1987-90</u>
Fiscal Technician II (Assistant Buyer), Department of
Corrections, Laramie, Wyoming

<u>1985-87</u>
Administrative Assistant, Purchasing Department, Q-Mart
Corporation, Casper, Wyoming

<u>1984-85</u>
Sales Clerk, Q-Mart, Casper, Wyoming

JOB SKILLS

Skilled in all aspects of purchasing including quality
control, bidding, acquisition of capital equipment and
records management

Experienced in using personal computers and various office
equipment

Skilled in vendor selection, inventory and supplier
relations

Experienced in dealing with international purchasing
practices

EDUCATIONAL BACKGROUND

Completed 30 credit hours at Casper College including
Principles of Purchasing I and II, 1984-87 (enrolled on
part-time basis)

Graduate, East Casper High School, Casper, Wyoming, 1984

REFERENCES provided on request

Laurin Richards
151 Cave Spring Road
Providence, RI 02840
(401) 555-9210

Career Objective

Challenging position in municipal government, state government or non-profit organization

Educational Background

B.S., University of Rhode Island
M.P.A. (Master of Public Administration), Villanova University
Additional courses in business administration completed at Penn State and
    Rutgers University (15 semester hours)

Work Experience

Have served eight years in city administration including positions as project development specialist and assistant city manager.

Have demonstrated outstanding skills in proposal development, project management and other tasks related to city planning and administration.

Current Position

Assistant City Manager
City of Providence
Providence, Rhode Island

Full work history available on request

References

References will be provided on request.

RESUME
Allison Wynn
321 Kaplan Avenue, South
Louisville, KY 40232
(502) 555-4320

EMPLOYMENT HISTORY:

1992-1996   Copy Editor, National Archives and
                 Records Administration, Washington, DC

Duties: Performed general copy-editing duties required for
publication of the <u>Federal Register</u>, a massive compilation
(averaging 50,000 pages annually) of public regulations and
legal notices issued by Federal agencies. Reviewed and
revised materials prior to publication. Consulted with
agency contacts in clarifying technical details or verbal
ambiguities. Reason for leaving: relocated due to job
transfer of spouse.

1988-1992   Editorial Assistant, National Science
                 Foundation, Washington, DC

Duties: Performed general editorial duties. Assisted in
editing reports, newsletters, requests for proposals and
other publications.

EDUCATION:

B.A., Elon College
Major: English

SPECIAL SKILLS

Highly versatile editor and writer

Adept at desktop publishing and use of word processing
     software

Competent photographer

REFERENCES:

Available on Request

**RESUME OF
ROBERT E. JOHNSON**

1802 King Street, SW
Alexandria, VA 22314
(703) 555-6984

EXPERIENCE

<u>1992-Present</u>
    Capital Markets Specialist
    Office of the Comptroller of the Currency, Federal Deposit
        Insurance Corporation
    Washington, DC

    Duties: In this position, I am responsible for analyzing practices related
    to risk-based capital standards of banking and bank holding companies.
    I am also involved in interpreting and implementing government policies
    and procedures related to capital standards.

<u>1989-92</u>
    Account Specialist
    Charles, White and Associates
    New York, New York

    Duties: Provided client assistance in a variety of areas, with emphasis
    on bilateral netting arrangements and derivative contracts related to
    equities.

<u>Summer, 1988</u>
    Student Intern
    Stinson College Fund, Inc.
    New York, NY

    Duties: Provided general assistance in client support.

EDUCATION

    M.B.A., Columbia University, 1989
    B.S., New York University, 1987

                                        Page 1 of 2

Johnson, 2

Major: Finance
Minor: Economics
Honors: Phi Beta Kappa; honor graduate; member of numerous student
    organizations

SPECIAL SKILLS

Excellent analytical skills

Advanced computer skills

Highly skilled in both written and oral communication

Strong "team player" and advocate of cooperative efforts in achieving
organizational goals

REFERENCES

Available on request

Winston P. Church
Valley View Lane Apartments, No. 11-B
21 East Maple Street
Montgomery, AL 36195
(334) 555-0537

OBJECTIVE

A position in auditing or financial management

EDUCATION

B.S. Alabama State University, 1990
    Major: Accounting

A.S. Ayers State Technical College, 1987

EXPERIENCE

Auditor, Alabama Department of Finance and Administration,
Montgomery, Alabama, 1990-95

Duties:

- Conducted field audits of state agencies and sub-
    units of agencies

- Examined financial and program records

- Wrote audit reports

- Communicated audit findings to agencies and state
    officials

Fiscal Technician, Alabama State University, Montgomery,
Alabama, 1985-90

Duties:

- Assisted in general fiscal management within the
    college's business office, including accounts
    payable, inventory and maintenance of departmental
    budgets.

- Played key role in designing computerized budget
    management system

                                          page 1 of 2

SPECIAL RECOGNITIONS

C.P.A.

Certified C.P.R. instructor

Outstanding Young Man of America, 1991

VOLUNTEERISM

Volunteer Firefighter

Special Olympics Volunteer

REFERENCES
PROVIDED
ON
REQUEST

JANIS PAYNE-BISHOP
506 Woodbury Lane
Bloomington, IN 47404
(812) 555- 5845

OBJECTIVE: Challenging administrative position requiring skills in program coordination and personnel management

CURRENT POSITION: Coordinator, J.J. Harris Regional Center for Single Parents/Homemakers

Have performed a wide range of duties in coordinating a Federally funded program providing support services for over 150 single parents and homemakers annually

--Supervised four employees

--Developed and disseminated information regarding the Center and its services

--Interviewed prospective clients

--Performed outreach and recruitment activities

--Acted as liaison with high schools, community service agencies and industries to inform them of information pertaining to the Center

--Supervised counseling and advising activities for program participants

--Prepared and monitored the Center's budget

--Supervised collection and maintenance of records documenting client eligibility and services provided for all program participants

--Evaluated project activities, documented results and complied with Federal reporting requirements

PRIOR WORK EXPERIENCE

Eight years of experience as a vocational counselor in

1 of 2

Payne-Bishop, 2

schools and job training programs. Complete details
available on request.

EDUCATION

B.S., Ohio University, Athens, Ohio, 1983
Major: Psychology

Additional courses completed at Indiana University in
counseling and business management.

REFERENCES

Complete reference information will be provided on request.

TOVANYA MARTIN

Address:
33 Park Street
Anchorage, AK 99513
(907) 555-6485

EDUCATION & TRAINING

Diploma in Office Systems Technology,
Anchorage Technical School

Additional training through completion of short-term courses
and seminars

PROFESSIONAL EXPERIENCE

1992-Present	Executive Secretary, Alaska State Office, U.S. Bureau of Land Management, Anchorage, Alaska
1989-1992	Secretary Senior, Alaska State Office, U.S. Bureau of Land Management
1987-89	Secretary, Advertising Department, <u>Juneau Empire</u> Newspaper

SKILLS/COMPETENCIES

Highly experienced in operating various types of office
equipment

Proficient in typing/word processing, averaging more than 70
words per minute. Familiar with several word processing and
office management software programs

Highly efficient in maintaining correspondence records and
filing systems

Skilled in telephone management, customer/client relations
and maintaining efficient oral and written communications,
both internal and external

REFERENCES

Available on request

TIMOTHY ARRINGTON   255 Falcolner Street
                                         Apartment 8-A
                                         Columbus, OH 43215
                                         (614) 555-1228

OBJECTIVE: A challenging position in recreation management

RELEVANT SKILLS AND EXPERIENCE

    Highly experienced in various aspects of planning and
    implementing recreation programs

    Experienced in athletics, aquatics, and outdoor
    adventure and interpretive service programming

    Flexible in reaching children, youths and adult
    audiences

    Effective in supervising subordinates, including part-
    time and volunteer workers

    Highly knowledgeable of effective marketing techniques

    Experienced in budgeting and fund management

    Experienced in developing community partnerships and
    making maximum use of resources

WORK HISTORY

    Assistant Recreation Director, City of Columbus, 1992-
        present

    Recreation Supervisor, City of Columbus, 1990-92

    Program Coordinator, Marietta Recreation Department,
        Marietta, Ohio 1987-90

EDUCATION

    B.S., The Ohio State University, 1987
    Major: Physical Education
    Minor: Recreation Management
    Member, Varsity Track Team

REFERENCES ON REQUEST

GLORIA MELENDEZ   21 North Carter Avenue
                                       Oakland, CA 94613
                                       (415) 555-3011

Career Objective   A POSITION IN GRANT DEVELOPMENT,
                         FEDERAL RELATIONS, PROGRAM MANAGEMENT OR
                         RELATED AREA

Professional Experience

- Served in grant services, City of Oakland, 1985-95.
  Specialized in writing grant proposals, completing
  grant reports and managing special projects supported
  by Federal and state funds.

- Performed wide range of tasks in proposal
  development, from idea development to completion of
  finished proposals. Worked independently and also in
  teams in joint proposals with county government,
  school systems and other local organizations.

- Played a direct role in winning more than $10
  million annually in grant funding

- Served as project director for more than fifteen
  externally funded projects

- Earned special certificate of appreciation from City
  Council for excellence in job performance

Public Service

Taught grant-writing seminars for local community college

Served as volunteer consultant for United Way agencies on
proposal development and project management

Served as field reader, U.S. Department of Education,
Washington, D.C. and U.S. Department of Energy, Oakland,
California

Education

Successfully completed special six-month program in proposal

Page 1 of 2

Melendez, 2

development offered by University of California system.

Earned Bachelor's Degree in political science, University of Oregon, 1985.

Completed additional courses in public administration, University of San Francisco, 1990-93.

Special Skills/Knowledge

Highly skilled in computer use

Highly competent in program evaluation design

Proven research skills

Excellent writing ability

References on Request

Alex Ni
122 Pine Avenue South
Sacramento, CA 95814
(916) 555-4650 (voice)
(916) 555-0907 (fax)

Summary of Qualifications

Highly experienced in providing health care services for state employees. Skilled in dealing with a wide spectrum of clients. Highly respectful and conscious of health care needs of individual employees while cognizant of organizational needs and constraints. Skilled both in clinical practices and administrative functions.

Accomplishments

Developed computerized system for storing and retrieving employee health records.

Improved reporting system for accident reports. Reduced average time for report processing by 40 percent.

Implemented improved program of health education seminars and activities which received "good" or "excellent" ratings from over 90 percent of participants.

Employment History

Public Health Nurse, State of California, 1985-Present.

> Department of Social Services, 1985-86.
> Department of Corrections, 1986-Present.

Duties: Evaluate physical condition of employees or potential employees

Plan and review clinical services

Treat work-related injuries (under guidance of physician) and work to reduce absenteeism

Review accident reports, analyze causes of accidents and recommend measures for accident

page 1 of 2

Ni, 2

reductions and related educational programs

Develop and implement employee education programs regarding health and safety

Order medical supplies and maintain inventory

Provide information to insurance companies regarding employees' medical status

Staff Nurse, St. Andrews Hospital, Stockton, Arizona, 1984-85.

Duties: Performed general nursing functions as floor nurse

Education/Certifications

B.S.N., Arizona State College, 1984.

Associate Degree, Pima Community College, 1982.

Registered Nurse.

References provided on request

Caretta L. Jones
22 Fremont Circle
Arlington, VA 22204
(703) 555-8668

Educational Background

J.D., University of Pennsylvania

B.A., Washington and Jefferson College, Washington, PA
History major, English minor
Magna Cum Laude graduate

Experience

Six years of experience as a staff attorney for the United
States International Trade Commission, Washington, DC.

Areas of Special Interest

*International Trade

*Regulatory development and interpretation

*Import regulations

*Legal aspects of exporting

Accomplishments

*Played key role in developing rules of origin (and
    later in modifications) for North American Free
    Trade Agreement

*Assisted in comprehensive revision of policies
    regarding anti-dumping and countervailing duty
    reviews

*Assisted in conducting numerous import investigations

References on request

Ray J. Blankman // 2120 Telegraph Road // Alexandria, VA 22310 // (703) 555-5220

Experience

1990-Present
Special Projects Officer, U.S. Agency for International Development (USAID), Bureau for Africa

1988-1990
Project Officer, USAID, Bureau for Africa and the Caribbean

1986-1988
Staff Associate, U.S. Chamber of Commerce

Special Skills

Skilled in project management and coordination

Fluent in French; reading knowledge of Spanish

Widely traveled and highly experienced in international affairs

Familiar with economic development trends/issues/strategies

Skilled in oral and written communications

Education

B.A. Sienna College
    Major: French
    Minor: Economics

M.A., Rockefeller University
    Major: Political Science

Additional short-term training through agency seminars/classes

References

Available on request

RESUME

William Burns
22 Wilson Lake Lane
Denver, CO 80210
(303) 555-2689
(303) 555-9880 (fax)

EMPLOYMENT HISTORY

1993-Present   Mine Inspector
                U.S. Mine Safety and Health Administration
                Denver, Colorado
                Chief coverage areas: Colorado, Wyoming

1985-93   Mine Inspector
                Mine Safety and Health Administration
                Beckley, West Virginia
                Chief coverage areas: Virginia, West
                Virginia, Kentucky

1980-84   Coal Miner
(summers)   Appalachian Energy, Inc.
                Morgantown, West Virginia

AREAS OF EXPERTISE

        Expert knowledge of safe mining practices

        Thorough familiarity with Federal safety regulations

        Experience in both surface and underground mining

        Proven human relations skills

        Excellent report writing skills

EDUCATION

B.S., West Virginia University, 1984
Major: Mining Technology

Burns, 2 of 2

Minor: Geology

Additional studies:
    West Virginia University
    Colorado School of Mines
    MSHA continuing education programs

REFERENCES

Available on Request

Erica Cox
P.O. Box 9060
213 North Wilson Avenue
Portland, OR 97232
(503) 555-6143

Employment Objective

Position as an administrative assistant, executive secretary
or similar role requiring professionalism and proven office
management skills

Experience

Seven years experience with the U.S. Bureau of Indian
Affairs, Portland Area Office, as a secretary serving the
Irrigation and Power Branch.

Duties included providing general secretarial support for
branch dealing with irrigation and power projects of
Flathead Reservation and other projects and activities
affecting Indian land.

Left position due to family relocation to East Coast.

Strengths

Highly effective office management skills

Accurate, speedy word processing capabilities

Effective communication skills

Extremely productive, task-oriented work style

Reliable transcription, note-taking, filing and record-
    keeping skills

High level of dependability, discretion and professionalism

Page 1 of 2

Cox, Page 2

Education

Certificate, Western Business College, Portland, Oregon, 1988

Diploma, Fulton Lewis High School, Portland, Oregon, 1987 (business track)

Memberships

Portland Secretarial Association (vice president for programming, 1994-95)

Big Sisters of America

Honors

Outstanding Secretarial Student, Western Business College, 1988

Secretary of the Interior's "You Make a Difference Award", 1993

References

References and additional background information, including typing and word processing samples, available on request.

Thurmond R. Chaffin
1972 Jaggerton Drive
St. Paul, MN 55101
(612) 555-6474

Summary of Qualifications

Highly experienced welder with track record of efficient, dependable service. Skilled in various welding techniques and applications. Certified by American Society of Mechanical Engineers.

Experience

Six years of experience as a welder with the Minnesota Department of Highways.

Bulk of experience has been in bridge construction and improvement.

Also experienced in welding for equipment repair, signage construction and other purposes.

Educational Background

Completed 24 credit hours in welding courses, Madison Area Technical College, Madison, Wisconsin.

Courses completed included:

    Oxyacetylene Welding and Cutting
    Arc Welding I and II
    Welding Metallurgy
    Welding Drawing and Interpreting
    Semi-automatic Welding Processes
    Visual Testing
    Inert Gas Welding
    Welding Quality Control

Graduate, Washington High School, Madison, Wisconsin

page 1 of 2

Chaffin, Page 2

Certifications/Memberships

Member, American Welding Society

Hold ASME (American Society of Mechanical Engineers) Code, Section IX, Welding and Brazing Qualifications

References

Complete references information will be provided on request

Lucy S. Joyner-Casey   21 Jefferson Lane
                                  Bethesda, MD 21228
                                  (301) 555-8681

CAREER OBJECTIVE: A position in technical writing or
related field

EXPERIENCE

- Technical Publications Writer, National Institute for
  Mental Health, Bethesda, Maryland, 1991-Present

- Technical Writer, Bio-Z Corporation, Columbus, Ohio,
  1989-91

- Publications Assistant (part-time position), College
  of Health Sciences, The Ohio State University,
  Columbus, Ohio, 1988-89

SELECTED PROFESSIONAL ACCOMPLISHMENTS

- Accomplished writer and editor with demonstrated
  flexibility in covering a wide range of subjects

- Principal author of more than 100 articles, brochures,
  manuals and other publications

- Contributing writer of more than 200 technical
  publications

- Cited by superiors for excellent job performance

- Winner of several awards for writing excellence
  including NIMH "Wordsmith" award

EDUCATIONAL BACKGROUND

B.S., The Ohio State University, 1989

    Major: Mass Communications

    Minor: Technical Writing

                                              1 of 2

Joyner-Casey   Page 2

Courses in major and minor included:

    Scientific Writing
    Graphic Design Principles
    Newswriting I and II
    Technical and Scientific Editing
    Public Relations Writing

Also completed several courses in biological sciences

SPECIAL SKILLS/KNOWLEDGE

Familiar with various types of word processing and desktop publishing software

Skilled in using the Internet and other applications of computer communications

Competent photographer

Skilled in basics of layout and design applications

REFERENCES AND WRITING SAMPLES AVAILABLE ON REQUEST

ANGELA ROMANO

<u>Address</u>:

421 White Street
Buffalo, NY 14222
(716) 555-9587

PROFESSIONAL SUMMARY

Experienced counselor with special emphasis on substance abuse counseling

WORK EXPERIENCE

1993-Present	Counselor, Buffalo Mental Health Services, Buffalo, New York
1991-93	Counselor, Buffalo City Schools, Buffalo, New York
1990-91	Mental Health Assistant, Buffalo Mental Health Services (Part-time)

EDUCATION

B.S. Buffalo State College, 1991
    Major: Counseling
    Minor: Psychology

A.S., Erie Community College, 1989
    Curriculum: Mental Health Assistant: Alcohol Counseling

SPECIAL SKILLS/CERTIFICATIONS

Fully certified by State of New York through comprehensive examination process

Skilled in various counseling areas, with extensive experience in problems related to drug and alcohol abuse

Active speaker for youth organizations and civic groups

REFERENCES

Provided on request

Fatima Lehar
20 South Harrison
Austin, TX 78704
(512) 555-2917

OBJECTIVE

A challenging position requiring advanced graphic design and
illustration skills

RELATED SKILLS AND EXPERIENCE

- Seven years of experience in graphic design and
  illustration

- Skilled in developing designs/illustrations for
  various applications including slide shows,
  brochures, magazines and newsletters

- Familiar with computerized graphics techniques as well
  as traditional drawing and other design methods

- Flexible in completing designs based on
  suggestions/requests by others as well as
  developing design concepts independently

- Diligent and task-oriented; able to handle heavy work
  load and undertake several projects simultaneously

PROFESSIONAL BACKGROUND

1989-Present   Graphic Artist, Texas Department
                of Education, Austin, Texas

Responsible for completing a wide range of graphics projects
in support of curriculum development, special projects,
production of publications and other efforts as a part of
the state department of education's instructional support
office. Promoted from Graphic Artist A to Graphic Artist B,
1994.

EDUCATION

A.S., Austin Community College, 1989. Major: Graphic
Communications.

REFERENCES PROVIDED ON REQUEST

```
SEAN P. SMITH, JR.
3397 NORTH PENNINGTON
DEARBORN, MI 48127
(313) 555-8408
```

Objective

A challenging position in fire safety or related area

Work Background

1992-95   Fire Chief, Dearborn Fire Department,
          Dearborn, MI

1981-92   Fire Officer, Dearborn Fire Department

1978-81   Security Guard, Ford Motor Company

1975-78   Infantryman, United States Army

Experience/Skills

Skilled in leadership and personnel management

Experienced in all aspects of fire fighting

Knowledgeable in fire prevention and safety techniques

Skilled in effective public relations strategies

Education

Associate in Applied Science (AAS)
Henry Ford Community College
Dearborn, Michigan, 1982

Major: Fire Protection Technology
Completed courses included:

    Fire Prevention and Protection
    Fire Protection and Alarm Systems
    Building Construction and Fire Hazards
    Fire Operations Strategy
    Legal Aspects of Fire Protection
    Chemistry of Hazardous Materials

Page 1 of 2

Smith, Page 2

Additional training through various state and local
firefighting courses/continuing education sessions

Graduate, Wilson High School, Detroit, Michigan, 1975

Community Service

Youth league football coach

Frequent speaker on fire safety and related issues

References

Available on request

CHRISTEN BAILEY
344 Elm Street
Paramus, NJ 07652
(201) 555-3080

PROFESSIONAL EXPERIENCE

Four years of experience in city management, including service as Assistant City Manager

JOB DUTIES

- Assisted City Manager in various aspects of city administration

- Planned City Council meetings and prepared agendas and follow-up documentation

- Assisted in budget development and fiscal management

- Coordinated city zoning program

- Wrote grant proposals for submission to state and Federal funding sources

- Assisted in comprehensive program of economic development

- Assisted in supervising clerical staff

EDUCATION

B.S. Rutgers University
Major: Public Administration

M.S. in progress, Rutgers University (21 semester hours completed)

REFERENCES

Available on request

Rolanda Anderson
1121 Peach Tree Estates
Washington, DC 20071
(202) 555-9847

Career Goal   POSITION IN MEDICAL RECORDS OR A RELATED
FIELD

Experience

Over ten years of service as a medical records technician. Served as a civilian employee at Walter Reed Army Hospital. In this capacity, I performed a variety of tasks including:

- Made patient room assignments

- Processed patient admission and discharge records

- Performed typing and word processing of patient records

- Filed medical records and assisted in maintaining efficient system of record-keeping

Work History

1986-96 Medical Records Technician, Walter Reed Army Hospital

1985-86 Office Assistant, Office of Dr. Weldon Jones (private practice)

Education

Diploma, American Business College, 1985

References

Will be provided on request

**RESUME OF
COLLIN K. ROBINSON**

22 College Heights Townhomes
Dover, Delaware 19903
(302) 555-7470 (voice)
(302) 555-2098 (fax)

EXPERIENCE

1993-96   Assistant City Attorney
            City of Dover
            Dover, Delaware

            Duties:

            ▪Provided legal counsel and representation for city government,
                specializing in civil law.

            ▪Represented elected and appointed officials, commissions and
                departments in litigation and other legal matters.

            ▪Drafted ordinances, resolutions, contracts and other
                documents.

            ▪Provided general assistance to City Attorney.

1990-92   Staff Attorney
            City of Philadelphia
            Philadelphia, Pennsylvania

            Duties: Provided general legal support with emphasis on civil law.

EDUCATION

B.A., Thiel College, 1987
        Major: History

1 of 2

Robinson, 2

Minor: Political Science
Honors/Activities: President of student government association, <u>summa cum laude</u> graduate, editor of college newspaper

J.D., Villanova University, 1990
Graduated with honors

AFFILIATIONS/MEMBERSHIPS

Delaware Bar Association

Pennsylvania Bar Association

American Bar Association

Association of Trial Lawyers of America

VOLUNTEERISM/COMMUNITY SERVICE

Legal Services volunteer

Member, Special Olympics Planning Team

REFERENCES

Available on request

Melissa Fonstadt   5560 W. 30th Street
                                     Indianapolis, IN 46206
                                     (317) 555-8920

EXPERIENCE

1993-Present   Benefits Coordinator
                City of Indianapolis
                Indianapolis, Indiana

1990-93   Personnel Technician
                City of Indianapolis

1989-90   Payroll Clerk
                Davis Manufacturing
                Gary, Indiana

SPECIAL SKILLS

Skilled in all aspects of benefits coordination including health insurance, pension funds and other benefits

Highly skilled in technical applications of benefit plans and other aspects of personnel/payroll functions

Adept at human relations including explaining benefits to new employees and dealing with problems and changes in benefits

Effective in using computers and other office equipment

EDUCATION

Associate Degree, Indiana Vocational-Technical College, Gary, Indiana

REFERENCES AVAILABLE ON REQUEST

Debra Aguiles
207 Congress Avenue
Montpelier, VT 05620
(802) 555-1626

OBJECTIVE: Challenging position requiring excellent skills in oral communication

JOB STRENGTHS:

Highly developed communication skills

Strong interpersonal skills

Proven reliability and dependability

WORK EXPERIENCE

1994-Present   Switchboard Operator
State Department of Education
Montpelier, Vermont

1993-94   Switchboard Operator
Vermont Department of Health
Burlington, Vermont

1991-93   Telemarketing Specialist
Bankcard Services, Inc.
Burlington, Vermont (part-time)

EDUCATION

Associate in Arts, Champlain College, 1993

Currently enrolled as part-time student, University of Vermont

REFERENCES

Complete reference information available

Lucy A. Kim, D.V.M.
38 Parkway Estates
Riverdale, MD 99258
(301) 555-1127

Employment Objective

Full-time position in private veterinary medicine practice

Experience

1994-Present   U.S. Animal and Plant Health Inspection Service
Riverdale, Maryland

Position: Staff Veterinarian

Duties:

Inspecting animals imported into the United States

Performing tests and treatments as needed

Completing reports regarding health condition of imported
animals

1994-Present   Pratt Animal Clinic
Riverdale, Maryland

Duties:

On a part-time (weekend) basis, performing general
veterinary services including surgeries

Page 1 of 2

Kim   Page 2

Education

D.V.M., 1994
University of Maryland

B.S., 1990
Frostburg State University

Memberships

American Veterinary Association

Maryland Veterinary Association

References

Available on request

JACK C. McHALE   1605 W. Front Street
                                      Baltimore, MD 21222
                                      (410) 555-7292

OBJECTIVE: A challenging position in research or research administration

EDUCATION

> B.S., University of North Carolina, Chapel Hill, North Carolina, 1983
>   Major: Psychology
>   Minor: Sociology
>   G.P.A.: 3.75 (4.0 scale)
>
> M.S. in Psychology, Iowa State University, Ames, Iowa, 1985
>   3.9 grade average
>
> Ph.D. in Psychology, Ohio State University, Columbus, Ohio, 1988
>   Area of Specialization: Psychology of Aging
>   Dissertation: <u>The Effectiveness of Three Visualization
>   Techniques In Reducing Stress In Nursing Home Residents</u>

PROFESSIONAL EXPERIENCE

National Institute on Aging, 1991-Present

> Position: Research Associate
>
> Duties: Conducting research studies. Designing research instruments. Collecting and analyzing data. Assisting in writing NIA reports.
>
> Research interest: Psychological aspects of stress in the aged.

Ohio Department of Social Services, 1988-91

> Position: Staff Psychologist
>
> Duties: Conducted research as part of Federally funded, state-level

page 1 of 2

program on status of senior citizens. Completed field studies and assisted in assembling project data. Performed some clinical duties.

PUBLICATIONS

Several publications in refereed journals including <u>APA Journal</u> and <u>Gerontology</u>. Complete list available.

AWARDS/RECOGNITIONS

Outstanding Psychology Student, 1983

Graduated <u>summa cum laude</u>

Recipient of Hawkeye Fellowship, Iowa State University, 1983-84 and 1984-85

MEMBERSHIPS

American Psychological Association

Society of Gerontological Research

REFERENCES AVAILABLE ON REQUEST

Patricia Howell   3347 E. Walker Circle, NW
Washington, DC 20036
(202) 555-4136 (voice)
(202) 555-6602 (fax)

PROFESSIONAL EXPERIENCE

1989-Present   Staff Photographer, United States Information Agency,
Washington, DC

1986-89   Photographic Assistant, <u>The Washington Times</u>,
Washington, DC

Highly skilled in various aspects of professional photography including
both color and black-and-white photography, illustrative photography,
photojournalism, portrait photography, darkroom techniques and
microphotography. Flexible in working with writers, editors and others through a
teamwork approach to produce highest possible quality results. Reliable in
meeting deadlines. Experienced in working independently to choose
appropriate subjects for journalistic purposes.

EDUCATION

Bachelor of Arts, Virginia State University, Petersburg, Virginia, 1986.

Major: Graphic Communication

Minor: Art History

Member of student newspaper staff; work also appeared in campus literary
magazine.

Member, Tau Lambda Tau Honor Society

REFERENCES ON REQUEST

Maureen Kelly
8 Shropshire Place · Gainesville, Florida 32601 · (904) 555-7164

Summary Resume

Education

Associate in Applied Science, Daytona Beach Community College, 1992
      Major: Pharmacy Technology
      Grade point average: 3.8

Professional Experience

      Pharmacy Technician
      VA Medical Center
      Gainesville, Florida
      1992-95

In this position, I performed pharmacy duties requiring attention to detail, reliability and dependability. Routine tasks included:

      Prepared and dispensed drugs in accordance with standard laws and procedures, under the supervision of a pharmacist

      Transcribed physician orders

      Prepared intravenous fluids

      Assisted in maintaining inventory of pharmaceutical supplies

      Maintained patient profile records and prepared bulk information

Received excellent performance evaluations. Vacated position due to relocation.

References

Available on request.

CARLA M. PEREZ
674 Rockbridge Road
Greenville, SC 26101
(803) 555-2624 (voice)
(803) 555-5402 (fax)

CAREER OBJECTIVE: A challenging role in employment counseling or related area

PROFESSIONAL BACKGROUND

South Carolina Employment Commission, 1982-Present

Job Title: Vocational Counselor

RELATED SKILLS AND EXPERIENCE

- Experienced with all aspects of vocational and employment counseling

- Flexible in dealing with clients from different age groups and socio-economic backgrounds

- Skilled in working with groups as well as providing individual counseling

- Adept in resume development and assistance in credential preparation

- Skilled in computerized job search processes and related computer applications

EDUCATION

Associate Degree
Greenville Technical College
Greenville, South Carolina

1 of 2

Perez, 2 of 2

Concentration: Social Services Administration

Additional courses completed at Furman University and University of South Carolina-Spartanburg (including fifteen semester hours in counseling)

MEMBERSHIPS

American Counseling Association

Upstate Society of Counseling Professionals

REFERENCES AVAILABLE ON REQUEST

CATHERINE P. LINLEY
142 Lighthouse Drive
Tacoma, WA 98467
(206) 555-3771

OBJECTIVE

A challenging position in human resources or personnel administration

PROFESSIONAL EXPERIENCE

1992- Present	Director of Human Resources City of Tacoma Tacoma, Washington
1990-92	Human Resources Officer City of Tacoma
1988-90	Assistant Personnel Officer Bellevue Public School District Bellevue, Washington
1985-86	Personnel Assistant Bellevue School District

EDUCATION

B.S., University of Puget Sound, 1988
Major: Business Administration
Minor: Management Science
Honors: Graduated cum laude; listed on dean's list five semesters

AFFILIATIONS

American Society for Training and Development

Washington Organization of Human Resource Officers

Page 1 of 2

Linley, Page 2 of 2

SPECIAL INTERESTS

Affirmative Action

Employee Counseling

Legal Aspects of Human Resource Administration

Employee Evaluation Methods

Coordination of Benefits

Computer Applications in Personnel Management

VOLUNTEERISM

Tacoma Food Bank Volunteer

United Way Planning Committee

Active member of several Chamber of Commerce committees

REFERENCES

Available on request

TERRI OVERSTREET   2713 Maplewood Drive
San Diego, CA 92152
(619) 555-6759

Career Objective   A POSITION IN ELECTRONICS SERVICE, REPAIR OR
INSTALLATION

Professional Experience

1992-96
Electronics Engineer
Naval Command, Control and Ocean Surveillance Center, San Diego, California

As a civilian employee of the United States Navy, served as an electronics
development/test engineer. Specialized in working with the global position
system (GPS). Duties included the following:

- Completed wide range of tasks in servicing and installing GPS
  equipment and related electronic equipment

- Diagnosed equipment problems and identified equipment malfunctions

- Tested, serviced, and replaced system components of complex
  electronic equipment

- Maintained up-to-date knowledge of advancements in electronics

- Mastered use of a variety of tools, testing devices, and other types of
  equipment

1991-92

Repair Technician
Smith Electronics
Compton, California

Serviced and repaired computers, radios, and other electronic equipment

1 of 2

116

Overstreet, Page 2

Education

A.A.S., Compton Community College, Compton, California, 1991
Major: Electronics Engineering Technology

Completed nine semester hours in engineering at San Diego State University

Successfully completed several continuing education seminars and correspondence courses sponsored by U.S. Navy

References

Provided on request

ROBERTO MELENDEZ
108 Guthrie Street, Fairfax, VA 22030
(703) 555-6821

EMPLOYMENT OBJECTIVE

To obtain a position in broadcasting, narration or other area requiring strong oral communication skills

RELATED SKILLS AND EXPERIENCE

- Highly experienced in broadcasting

- Experienced in delivering both live and taped material

- Fluent in Spanish

- Highly flexible in adapting to varying work environments and situations

WORK BACKGROUND

1991-Present

U.S. Information Agency
Voice of America Program
Position: International Radio Broadcaster

Duties: Reading news and informational material for radio broadcast to countries outside the United States. Specialty in Spanish-language broadcasts.

1989-91

WXKY Radio
Richmond, Virginia
Position: News Reader

Duties: Read copy for local, national and international news.

Melendez, 2

Also presented public service announcements and assisted in developing
and presenting interview shows, ads and promos

1989-Present

Free-lance Talent

Provided narration for training films, educational videos, "infomercials"
and other productions

EDUCATIONAL BACKGROUND

B.S., University of Richmond, 1989
Major: Mass Communication
Minor: Public Relations
Active in numerous student activities including several roles with campus
radio station

REFERENCES WILL BE PROVIDED ON REQUEST

PEGGY M. DUVALL
18 Beechtree Court
Roanoke, VA 24022
(540) 555-3726

CAREER OBJECTIVE: A challenging role in nutrition or related area

BACKGROUND

> U.S. Veterans Administration, 1991-1996
> Virginia Veteran Care Center
> Roanoke, Virginia
> Position: Dietician

PROFESSIONAL EXPERIENCE

- Performed a wide range of duties in providing dietary planning for patients and other clients

- Prepared menus for general meal planning and preparation, as well as specialized menus for individual patients based on medical requirements

- Prepared educational materials for patients and their families regarding dietary needs/restrictions

- Performed other duties related to nutrition needs of patients

EDUCATION

Bachelor's Degree
University of Georgia
Athens, Georgia
Major: Human Nutrition

REFERENCES AVAILABLE ON REQUEST

MEREDITH FOSTER
11 West Club Boulevard
Des Moines, IA 50319
(515) 555-6477

CAREER OBJECTIVE

Desire a challenging position in budgeting or financial management

Professional Experience

Iowa Department of Public Health, Des Moines, Iowa, 1992-Present
Position: Budget Officer

Job tasks have included:

- Preparing departmental budgets
- Reviewing budget documents prepared by constituent agencies
- Monitoring financial transactions and maintaining current data
- Processing adjustments in approved budgets
- Developing and analyzing budgetary data

Indianola Municipal Government, Indianola, Iowa, 1990-91
Position: Financial technician
Duties included assisting in general financial management including accounts payable, budgeting and internal auditing

Education

B.S. Simpson College, 1992
Major: Finance

A.S., Des Moines Area Community College, 1989
Major: Business Management

References

Complete reference information available on request

Arthur C. Jackson

331 Andrews Drive
Germantown, MD 20874
(410) 555-7663

QUALIFICATIONS SUMMARY

Highly experienced manager familiar with government policies, procedures and practices as well as private sector business endeavors. Self-starter with strong organizational skills.

EXPERIENCE

U.S. Department of Energy, 1991-Present
Germantown, Maryland
Position: Assistant Program Manager

Duties: In this highly responsible position, I assist in coordinating management of more than $20 million annually in research grants to small businesses. Specific duties include:

- Maintaining control of more than 25 projects conducted by small businesses around the nation

- Assisting in the review of applications for funding

- Negotiating grant awards with successful applicants

- Monitoring progress of individual projects

- Maintaining contacts with principal investigators/project directors

- Developing statistical and narrative reports regarding program activities

U.S. Small Business Administration (SBA), 1988-91
Washington, DC
Position: Contract Officer

Resume, Jackson, 2

Duties: Assisted in executing and recording various contractual agreements with recipients of SBA awards.

U.S. Small Business Administration (SBA), 1985-88
Washington, DC
Position: Fiscal Management Assistant

Duties: Completed budgetary transfers and other financial transactions. Provided general assistance to senior contracting staff.

EDUCATIONAL BACKGROUND

B.S., Howard University, 1991
Major: Business
G.P.A. 3.75
(Attended full-time 1983-85; completed degree on part-time basis while employed)

SPECIAL SKILLS

- Skilled in use of spreadsheets and other computer applications
- Highly organized and effective in records management
- Good communication skills (both oral and written)
- Skilled in using various types of office equipment
- Highly accurate and analytical in working with financial data

REFERENCES AVAILABLE ON REQUEST

ALBERT H. CAVELLI, JR.
86 Newport Place
Woodbridge, VA 22192
(703) 555-1468

QUALIFICATIONS SUMMARY

EXPERIENCE

1993-Present	Assistant Program Director Division of International Programs National Science Foundation Arlington, Virginia
1990-93	Associate Professor of Physics The Pennsylvania State University State College, Pennsylvania
1986-90	Lecturer in Physics University of Essex Essex, England
1984-86	Research Associate Department of Physical Sciences University of Wisconsin

EDUCATION

Ph.D., University of Wisconsin, 1984

M. S., University of Illinois, 1982

B.S., Allegheny College, 1979

Cavelli, Page 1 of 2

Cavelli, Page 2 of 2

AREAS OF RESEARCH/PROFESSIONAL INTERESTS

Fluid Dynamics

Innovative methods of undergraduate science instruction

International education

PUBLICATIONS

Publications in several refereed journals including <u>Science</u>. Complete list available on request.

REFERENCES

Provided on request

Kenneth Krocak
1102 8th Avenue
Jackson, MS 39206
(601) 555-7842

Objective

A responsible position in security or related area

Experience

<u>1994-Present</u>

Director of Security
State Capitol Complex
Jackson, Mississippi

Duties:

>   Providing overall coordination of security for state
>   capitol building and surrounding buildings and grounds
>
>   Supervising a staff of nine security personnel
>
>   Evaluating security needs and planning appropriate
>   measures to insure maximum security for members of the
>   state legislature, staff and visitors
>
>   Anticipating security threats and reacting to problems
>   and potential problems
>
>   Assuring that all appropriate laws, policies and
>   procedures are followed by security staff
>
>   Hiring and evaluating security personnel
>
>   Completing security reports and other documents

<u>1992-94</u>

Assistant Director of Security
State Capitol Complex
Jackson, Mississippi

1 of 2

Krocak, 2 of 2

Duties:

>   Assisted director in coordinating security affairs.

>   Held primary responsibility for orienting new staff and maintaining employee work schedules.

1980-92

Military Police Officer
United States Army

Duties: Performed a wide range of security duties at several Army installations

Education

B.S., University of Georgia, 1988
G.P.A.: 3.3

Courses completed included Introduction to Criminal Justice, Criminal Procedures, Criminal Law, Abnormal Psychology, Criminology, Administration of Criminal Justice, Security Principles and Procedures, Criminal Investigation.

Additional training provided through U.S. Army training courses.

References

Provided on request

EARL A. BROWN
405 East Wilson Street
Helena, MT 59620
(406) 555-7607

EXPERIENCE

1993-Present   Director of Physical Facilities
                State Capitol Complex
                Helena, Montana

1986-93   Assistant Director of Physical Facilities
                State Capitol Complex
                Helena, Montana

1984-86   Supervisor of Custodial Services
                Montana University System Offices
                Helena, Montana

1980-84   Custodian
                Montana University System Offices

SKILLS/COMPETENCIES

Highly experienced, competent manager with a strong track
record in:

        Energy management

        Personnel supervision

        Construction and renovation

        Fire and safety standards

        Preventive maintenance

        Environmental health

        Customer service

REFERENCES

Available on request

ERIC BRYANT
21 Parker Place Apartments
Trenton, New Jersey 08650
(609) 555-0596

SUMMARY OF QUALIFICATIONS

WORK EXPERIENCE

1993-Present   U.S. Department of Agriculture, Food and
                     Nutrition Service (FNS)
                 Mid-Atlantic Region Office
                 Trenton, New Jersey

                 Position: Coordinator of Shipping and
                            Receiving

                 Duties: Coordinating all incoming and
                 outgoing mail, packages and other materials.
                 Responsibilities include staff supervision
                 and budget management.

1990-93   Mid-Atlantic Region Office, FNS

                 Position: Shipping Clerk

1987-90   Atrex Chemical Corporation
                 Jersey City, New Jersey

                 Position: Shipping/Receiving Clerk

EDUCATIONAL BACKGROUND

Certificate in Business Management
Hudson County Community College
Jersey City, New Jersey

REFERENCES

Reference information provided on request

Lisa Fain-Smith
4123 Derby Ridge Road
Frankfort, KY 40621
(502) 555-0274

OBJECTIVE

A position taking advantage of my skills and experience in interpreting for the hearing-impaired

EDUCATION

B.S. Kentucky State University, 1992
    Major: Liberal Studies
    Minor: Sign Communication

Certificate in American Sign Language (ASL), Jefferson Community College, 1993. Successfully completed preparation course and passed state certification exam, 1993.

EXPERIENCE

Interpreter, Kentucky Department of Social Services, Frankfort, Kentucky 1993-Present

Duties: Provide interpreting services for social services clients. Train staff in basics of manual sign language. Provide interpreting both on individual and group basis.

SPECIAL SKILLS

Adept at all facets of communication via sign language. Fluent in American Sign Language.

Skilled in one-on-one communication.

Experienced in interpreting for various-sized groups in formal and informal situations

REFERENCES
PROVIDED
ON
REQUEST

Chapter Six

SAMPLE COVER LETTERS

SUSAN A. WOO
825 Riverdale Avenue
Fairfax, VA 22033
(703) 555-8057

Paul Robertson
Director of Personnel
Baltimore Community College
Baltimore, MD 21202

Dear Ms. Andrews:

Please accept the enclosed resume in application for
the position of Assistant Director of Computing Services as
announced September 1.

I believe my extensive background in computer
progamming and computing services meets or exceeds the
qualifications for this position. While employed with the
U. S. Department of Education, I have specialized in
performing duties very similar to those listed in your job
announcement.

In addition to my professional background, my deep
interest in education would be an asset in serving as a
member of your staff. I must admit excitement at the
prospect of working in a community college environment.

Please review the enclosed resume and call me at the
number listed above if you would like to discuss my interest
in this position or schedule an interview. I will be
available at your convenience.

Thank you for your consideration.

Sincerely,

Susan A. Woo

Winston P. Church
Valley View Lane Apartments, No. 11-B
21 East Maple Street
Montgomery, AL 36195
(334) 555-0537

Charles Ferguson, Director
Mississippi Department of Fianance and Administration
415 Lamar Street
Jackson, MS 39202

Dear Mr. Ferguson:

I understand that your office is considering expanding. I am an experienced and highly dependable auditor, and as such would like to apply for a position should one become available.

Enclosed is a copy of my resume. You will see that I have over ten years of experience in performing a variety of auditing and accounting tasks. This experience has prepared me well to take on further levels of responsibility.

If a position opens with your agency, I will appreciate the chance to submit an application. I will be glad to provide additional information by mail or telephone, or to come for an interview if invited.

Thank you for any consideration you might give me regarding possible employment. I look forward to talking with you.

Very truly yours,

Winston Church

Judy Anderson
333 St. Albans Drive,
Raleigh, NC 27695
(919) 555-2636

Sara Jane Tolbert, Director of Operational Support
Georgia State Department of Corrections
301 Haddock Tower
Atlanta, GA 30323

Dear Ms. Tolbert:

Thank you for talking with me today. I enjoyed our telephone conversation.

I am enclosing a copy of my resume, as you requested. This will provide you with more details regarding my qualifications.

You will see that I have a great deal of experience in maintaining computer networks and providing appropriate support. I am familiar with a wide range of equipment and software, and am a proven self-starter with an excellent work ethic.

I am available to meet with you in at your convenience to discuss your agency's needs for computing personnel, as well as my capabilities for fulfilling them. I will certainly appreciate the chance to apply for any appropriate position openings.

Thank you again for talking with me. I look forward to hearing from you.

                        Sincerely,

                        Judy Anderson

MARK A. BURNS
Apartment 24-C
Alpine Estates
Alexandria, VA 22314
(703) 555-3618

Mr. Edwardo Reyes, Director
Virginia Department of Personnel and Training
401 North Eighth Street
Richmond, VA 23240

Dear Mr. Reyes:

This is to inquire about employment opportunities with your agency. Enclosed is a resume outlining my qualifications.

I am a dependable, creative manager with a strong track record in human resource administration in a government setting. As my resume shows, my background includes appropriate experience and training for a wide variety of tasks related to personnel management.

I would be interested in any position consistent with my background and experience. Please let me know if you have any openings for which I might apply. I will be glad to provide additional details or meet with you for a personal interview.

Your consideration is appreciated. I look forward to talking with you.

Sincerely,

Mark A. Burns

Gregory Smith
323 Landview Place
Washington, DC 20002
(202) 555-3495

Marfesa Adams, Human Resources Coordinator
U.S. Small Business Administration
North Carolina District Office
201 North College Street
Charlotte, NC 28202

Dear Ms. Adams:

I am interested in the position of public information
director advertised in Sunday's edition of the <u>Washington
Post</u>. My resume is enclosed. I will also be glad to fill
out an application form if you will be so kind as to provide
one.

As you will see from the information provided, I have
extensive experience in public relations and public
information activities. I currently hold a position in this
area with the U.S. Department of Commerce.

I am considering relocating and your job announcement caught
my interest. I believe that my background provides a strong
match for the advertised position.

If you need more information or would like me to submit an
application form, please let me know.

Thank you very much for your consideration. I will look
forward to hearing from you.

              Yours truly,

              Gregory Smith

CATHERINE P. LINLEY
142 Lighthouse Drive
Tacoma, WA 98467

Ms. Patricia Linkous, Assistant Director
U.S. Department of Education
Region III Office
3500 Market Street
Philadelphia, PA 19104

Dear Ms. Linkous:

Please accept the enclosed resume and letters of recommendation in application for the human resources position vacancy recently annnounced at your agency.

As you will gather from my resume, I have a great deal of experience in human resource management. In fact, I believe that my professional background provides the ideal qualifications you are seeking.

If I need to submit a government application form or provide other details about my qualifications, please let me know. I will follow up promptly with any necesssary information.

I will be relocating to Philadelphia in the near future, and thus geography is not a factor in my availability. For the present, I can be reached at (206) 555-3771. You may reach me at any time through my voice mail service.

Thank you for your consideration. I look forward to your response.

Sincerely,

Catherine P. Linley

ANGELA ROMANO
421 White Street
Buffalo, NY 14222

Mr. Michael Russell
Ohio Department of Mental Health
30 East Broad Street
Columbus, Ohio 43266-0411

Dear Mr. Russell:

Enclosed is my resume for your consideration for any
suitable counselor openings within your agency. I would be
interested in applying for any such positions that may
become open in the near future.

I have had a great deal of experience in counseling,
especially in the area of substance abuse. I would be
interested in a role within that capacity that provides the
opportunity to apply my skills and training in a clinical or
administrative capacity.

I believe that my experience and strong work ethic will
allow me to make a significant contribution to your agency.
Please let me know if you would like more information about
my qualifications.

I hope you will consider me for any appropriate position
openings, and look forward to hearing from you. Thank you
for your consideration.

Sincerely yours,

Angela Romano

DON P. HARRELL
3229 Roanoke Street
Nashville, TN 37219
(617) 555-3215

Dr. Lorraine Kirk
National Institute of Allergy and Infectious Diseases
6003 Executive Boulevard
Bethesda, MD 20892

Dear Dr. Kirk:

Thank you for taking the time to talk with me yesterday about employment possibilities with your agency. Your enthusiasm about NIAID is obvious, and I am highly interested in following up on our conversation.

Enclosed for your review is a copy of my resume. You will see, as we discussed, that I have had appropriate experience here in Tennessee related to the position we discussed.

In addition to my training and experience, I am a hard worker who enjoys new challenges. I have excellent communication skills as well as strong organizational capabilities.

Please review my background and call me at the number listed above if you would like to talk further. I would be available for an interview at any time.

Thank you for your consideration.

Sincerely,

Don P. Harrell

Patricia Howell
3347 E. Walker Circle, NW
Washington, DC 20036
(202) 555-4136 (voice)
(202) 555-6602 (fax)

Mr. James R. Anderson, Publications Manager
National Endowment for the Humanities
420 K Street, SW
Washington, DC 20202

Dear Mr. Anderson:

As you may recall, I spoke with you last month regarding possible employment with your agency. I would now like to express my interest in employment at this time.

Enclosed is a copy of my resume for your perusal.
As you will note, I have had considerable experience as a professional photographer. It is my hope to build upon my background by taking on new types of assignments, preferably within a Federal agency such as NEH.

I would appreciate the opportunity to talk with you in person to discuss your agency's photographic needs and how I might help meet them. I would be happy to come to your office at any time either to talk informally, or to participate in a formal interview.

Please let me know if you would like samples of my work or other information. I look forward to hearing from you.

Sincerely yours,

Patricia Howell

TOVANYA MARTIN
33 Park Street
Anchorage, AK 99513
(907) 555-6485

Ms. Lauren Weddle, Director of Personnel Services
U.S. Small Business Administration
222 W. 8th Street
Anchorage, AK 99513

Dear Ms. Weddle:

It is my understanding that your agency employs a number of word processing specialists, administrative assistants, and other clerical and administrative support personnel. I have specialized in such functions while serving on the staff of the Bureau of Land Management here in Anchorage. Although I have enjoyed my service with this agency, I would like to take on the challenge of a new position.

Please see the enclosed copy of my resume. As you will see, I have a broad range of experience in providing office support services. I can offer excellent technical skills, outstanding communication capabilities, and the capacity to carry a heavy workload.

I would be most interested in discussing with you any opportunities for employment with your agency. Please contact me if you would like additional information.

Thank you for your consideration.

Sincerely,

Tovanya Martin

Allison Wynn
321 Kaplan Avenue, South
Louisville, KY 40232
(502) 555-4320

Brian Koczko, Director of Public Information
State Department of Natural Resources
1026 Capitol Center Drive
Frankfort, KY 40601-8204

Dear Mr. Koczko:

This is to inquire about possible employment with your agency. I have seen many of your publications, and am aware of the broad range of publications and public information services provided by your department. I would be very interested in joining your staff should a position become available.

My background includes diverse editorial experience with both the National Archives and Record Administration and the National Science Foundation. This has included performing various types of editorial and public information tasks.

Enclosed is a copy of my resume for your review. If you would like additional information, I would be glad to provide it. Please let me know if you would like for me to meet with you in person to discuss your employment needs.

Thank you for considering my resume. I hope to hear from you soon.

Sincerely,

Allison Wynn

Enclosure

Arthur C. Jackson
331 Andrews Drive
Germantown, MD 20874
(410) 555-7663

Ms. Alicia Gladden
Defense Supply Service
5200 Army Pentagon
Washington, DC 20310-5200

Dear Ms. Gladden:

Thank you for talking with me today about the program management position advertised in last Sunday's edition of <u>The Washington Post</u>. Please let me reiterate my interest in the position.

A copy of my resume is enclosed for your review. You will note that I have had significant experience in managing government programs and conducting related functions. My experience with the U.S. Department of Energy and the Small Business Administration has provided me a wealth of experience in this area.

After studying the description for the position at your agency, I believe that my background provides a solid match with your needs. Please let me know if you would like for me to complete an application form. I would also be happy to amplify on my qualifications and interests through a personal interview.

If you would like to discuss this matter, please contact me at your convenience. I shall look forward to hearing from you.

Sincerely,

Arthur C. Jackson

Enclosure: Resume

DAVID GOLDSTEIN, JR.
411 South Mason Street
Washington, DC 20002
(202) 555-3290

Roberto Salazar, Director of Administrative Services
Maryland Department of Public Safety
305 West Preston Street, Room 112
Baltimore, MD 21201

Dear Mr. Salazar:

I am submitting this letter in follow-up to our recent
conversation. As I indicated in our discussion, I would
appreciate being considered for the forensic technologist
position currently being advertised.

As the enclosed resume notes, I have significant experience
in evidence/forensics laboratory though my service with the
Federal Bureau of Investigation. Those with whom I have
worked have found me a thorough and dependable technologist.

I will appreciate your reviewing my background relative to
your requirements. If you would like more information,
please contact me. I look forward to hearing from you.

Sincerely,

David Goldstein, Jr.

NORA L. KLEIN
1426 Wilson Avenue
Hagerstown, MD 21741

Mr. Michael Yarborough
Grants and Contracts Division
U.S. Department of Energy
19901 Germantown Road
Germantown, MD 20874-1290

Dear Mr. Yarborough:

I would like to apply for the accounting position currently being advertised by your department. Thus I am sending the enclosed resume.

I have had a great deal of experience in performing a variety of accounting and financial management tasks. While serving with the National Institute of Health, I have gained first-hand exposure to a variety of financial processes and procedures. This experience has prepared me well for a wide range of accounting and financial management duties.

My strengths include excellent quantitative skills, thorough work habits, and strong capabilities in written and oral communication. I am a highly motivated and dedicated worker.

The enclosed resume outlines my background. If you would like me to complete an application form or provide more information, please contact me. I would be delighted to meet with you to discuss my qualifications in further detail.

Thank you for your consideration.

Sincerely,

Nora Klein

Phone (301) 555-4865

JERRIE P. SPANGLER
14-B Red Maple Village
Laramie, WY 82071
(307) 555-3541

Mr. Carl Phlegar
U.S. Commerce Department
National Oceanic and Atmospheric Administration
601 East 12th Street
Kansas City, MO 64106

Dear Mr. Phlegar:

Please accept this letter and the enclosed resume in application for the position of Procurement Specialist recently advertised by your agency.

My background in purchasing has provided me with a firm foundation in performing procurement functions and related tasks. I am highly experienced in following the strict standards required for government purchasing.

I would appreciate your reviewing the enclosed resume. Please let me know if I can become a part of your agency's future. I will be glad to provide any additional details you might require.

Your consideration is appreciated.

Sincerely yours,

Jerrie Spangler

Lucy S. Joyner-Casey

Mr. James Chao
Publications Department
National Science Foundation
4201 Wilson Boulevard
Arlington, VA 22230

Dear Mr. Chao:

I enjoyed our telephone conversation yesterday. Thank you
for taking the time to talk with me.

As we discussed, my background as a technical writer could
prove a significant asset should I join your staff. I
believe I would bring a fresh perspective to your
department, and could help in your quest to bring top
quality to NSF publications.

The enclosed resume provides important details about my
background. After you have reviewed it, please let me know
if you would like to discuss present or future needs of your
department, and how I might meet them.

Yours truly,

Lucy S. Joyner-Casey
21 Jefferson Lane
Bethesda, MD 21228
(301) 555-8681

Douglas A. Cozzins
113 Speer Street, North
Kansas City, MO 64153
(816) 555-5018

Ms. Patricia E. Thompson
General Services Administration
18th and F Streets, NW
Washington, DC 20405

Dear Ms. Thompson:

This letter and the enclosed resume are submitted in the event that you may have a position vacancy for a paralegal either in Washington or in your Kansas City office.

I have a solid background in paralegal services through my previous service with government agencies (see resume for details). Over the past eleven years, I have proven myself to be a diligent and resourceful worker.

Should a position be open now or in the near future, I would appreciate the opportunity to apply. My resume provides basic details regarding my background and experience; if additional details are needed, please contact me.

Thank you for considering my application. I would appreciate hearing from you.

Yours truly,

Douglas Cozzins

TINA ALLISON
P.O. Box 728
Milwaukee, WI 53217
(414) 555-3202

Roger Baggett, Director of Public Information
Iowa Department of Commerce
201 East Grand Avenue
Des Moines, IA 50309

Dear Mr. Baggett:

Please accept the enclosed resume and samples of my work in application for the position of Graphic Artist with your agency. I am responding to the position announcement appearing in the March 12 edition of the Sun Times.

I have worked successfully within the state government in Wisconsin, and am now interested in relocating to Iowa. I am highly skilled in a variety of graphic arts techniques, and could prove a valuable addition to your agency.

I would be happy to provide additional examples of my work. Of course, I would also appreciate an opportunity to meet with you in person and discuss the position more fully.

Please contact me if I can provide additional information. I look forward to the prospect of talking with you.

Yours sincerely,

Tina Allison

Hannah Sexton-Boyd
11 Bayview Drive
Apartment 22H
Honolulu, Hawaii 96825
(808) 555-3640

Ms. Anna L. Dean, Human Resources Manager
U.S. Small Business Administration
301 Ala Moana Boulevard, Room 2214
Honolulu, HI 96850-4981

Dear Ms. Dean:

I am submitting the enclosed resume for your consideration in the event that you need to add to your secretarial staff. As a highly skilled secretary, I would be available should you wish to add a dependable employee to your agency.

As my resume shows, my experience with the Hawaii Department of Education, as well as my educational training, has prepared me well to perform a wide variety of clerical and professional support tasks. I am energetic, highly motivated and dependable, and take great pride in providing work of excellent quality.

I would appreciate the opportunity to meet with you in person to discuss your agency's needs and how I might meet them. If you would like letters of recommendation or any other details, I would be glad to provide them.

Please let me know if additional details about my background are needed. Thank you for your consideration.

Yours truly,

Hannah Sexton-Boyd

Thomas Ryan
2249 Carolina Avenue
Atlanta, GA 30341
(404) 555-2128 (voice)
(404) 555-5578 (fax)

Mr. Thomas P. Parris
Director of Human Resources
Naval Research Laboratory
4555 Overlook Avenue, SW
Washington, DC 20375-5326

Dear Mr. Parris:

Please accept the enclosed resume in application for
the position of Assistant Director of Statistical Services
as announced September 1.

I believe my extensive background in statistics meets
or exceeds the qualifications for this position. While
employed with the Centers for Disease Control, I have
specialized in performing duties similar to those listed in
your job announcement.

In addition to my professional background, my deep
interest in military affairs would be an asset should I be
selected for this position. I must admit excitement at the
prospect of working in a setting contributing to our
nation's military readiness.

Please review the enclosed resume and call me at the
number listed above if you would like to discuss my interest
in this position or schedule an interview. I will be
available at your convenience.

Thank you for your consideration.

Sincerely,

Thomas Ryan

VGM CAREER BOOKS

CAREER DIRECTORIES
Careers Encyclopedia
Dictionary of Occupational Titles
Occupational Outlook Handbook

CAREERS FOR
Animal Lovers
Bookworms
Caring People
Computer Buffs
Crafty People
Culture Lovers
Environmental Types
Fashion Plates
Film Buffs
Foreign Language Aficionados
Good Samaritans
Gourmets
Health Nuts
History Buffs
Kids at Heart
Nature Lovers
Night Owls
Number Crunchers
Plant Lovers
Shutterbugs
Sports Nuts
Travel Buffs
Writers

CAREERS IN
Accounting; Advertising; Business;
Child Care; Communications;
Computers; Education;
Engineering;
the Environment; Finance;
Government; Health Care; High
Tech; International Business;
Journalism; Law; Marketing;
Medicine; Science; Social &
Rehabilitation Services

CAREER PLANNING
Beating Job Burnout
Beginning Entrepreneur
Career Planning & Development for
College Students &
Recent Graduates
Career Change
Careers Checklists
College and Career Success for
Students with Learning Disabilities
Complete Guide to Career Etiquette
Cover Letters They Don't Forget
Dr. Job's Complete Career Guide
Executive Job Search Strategies

Guide to Basic Cover Letter
Writing
Guide to Basic Résumé Writing
Guide to Internet Job Searching
Guide to Temporary Employment
Job Interviewing for College
Students
Joyce Lain Kennedy's Career Book
Out of Uniform
Slam Dunk Résumés
The Parent's Crash Course in
Career Planning: Helping Your
College Student Succeed

CAREER PORTRAITS
Animals; Cars; Computers;
Electronics; Fashion;
Firefighting; Music; Nursing;
Sports; Teaching; Travel; Writing

GREAT JOBS FOR
Business Majors
Communications Majors
Engineering Majors
English Majors
Foreign Language Majors
History Majors
Psychology Majors

HOW TO
Apply to American Colleges and
Universities
Approach an Advertising Agency and
Walk Away with the Job You Want
Be a Super Sitter
Bounce Back Quickly After
Losing Your Job
Change Your Career
Choose the Right Career
Cómo escribir un currículum vitae
en inglés que tenga éxito
Find Your New Career Upon
Retirement
Get & Keep Your First Job
Get Hired Today
Get into the Right Business School
Get into the Right Law School
Get into the Right Medical School
Get People to Do Things Your Way
Have a Winning Job Interview
Hit the Ground Running in Your
New Job
Hold It All Together When You've
Lost Your Job
Improve Your Study Skills
Jumpstart a Stalled Career

Land a Better Job
Launch Your Career in TV News
Make the Right Career Moves
Market Your College Degree
Move from College into a
Secure Job
Negotiate the Raise You Deserve
Prepare Your Curriculum Vitae
Prepare for College
Run Your Own Home Business
Succeed in Advertising When all
You Have Is Talent
Succeed in College
Succeed in High School
Take Charge of Your Child's Early
Education
Write a Winning Résumé
Write Successful Cover Letters
Write Term Papers & Reports
Write Your College Application Essay

MADE EASY
Cover Letters
Getting a Raise
Job Hunting
Job Interviews
Résumés

OPPORTUNITIES IN
This extensive series provides
detailed information on nearly 150
individual career fields.

RÉSUMÉS FOR
Advertising Careers
Architecture and Related Careers
Banking and Financial Careers
Business Management Careers
College Students &
Recent Graduates
Communications Careers
Education Careers
Engineering Careers
Environmental Careers
Ex-Military Personnel
50+ Job Hunters
Government Careers
Health and Medical Careers
High School Graduates
High Tech Careers
Law Careers
Midcareer Job Changes
Re-Entering the Job Market
Sales and Marketing Careers
Scientific and Technical Careers
Social Service Careers
The First-Time Job Hunter

VGM Career Horizons
a division of *NTC Publishing Group*
4255 West Touhy Avenue
Lincolnwood, Illinois 60646–1975